Anger and Conflict
In The Workplace

Titles in the CareerSavvy Series™:

Anger and Conflict in the Workplace

100 Top Internet Job Sites

101 Hiring Mistakes Employers Make...and How to Avoid Them

Recruit and Retain the Best

The 100 Best Web Sites for HR Professionals

The Difficult Hire

Savvy Interviewing

The Savvy Resume Writer

Anger and Conflict In the Workplace

Spot the Signs, Avoid the Trauma

Lynne McClure, Ph.D.

IMPACT PUBLICATIONS
Manassas Park, Virginia

Library of Congress Cataloging-in-Publication Data

McClure, Lynne Falkin.

Anger and conflict in the workplace: spot the signs, avoid the trauma/ Lynne McClure.

p. cm.—(The career savvy series)

ISBN 1-57023-138-9 (alk. paper)

1. Violence in the workplace. 2. Anger. 3. Conflict management. I. Title. II. Series.

HF5549.5.E43 M389 2000
658.3'8—dc21 00-029546

Publisher: For information on Impact Publications, including current and forthcoming publications, authors, press kits, bookstore, and submission requirements, visit Impact's Web site: *www.impactpublications.com*

Publicity/Rights: For information on publicity, author interviews, and subsidiary rights, contact Media Relations: Tel. 703/361-7300 or Fax 703/335-9486.

Sales/Distribution: Bookstore sales are handled through Impact's trade distributor: National Book Network, 15200 NBN Way, Blue Ridge Summit, PA 17214, Tel. 1-800-462-6420. All other sales and distribution inquiries should be directed to the publisher: Sales Department, IMPACT PUBLICATIONS, 9104 Manassas Dr., Suite N, Manassas Park, VA 20111-5211, Tel. 703/361-7300, Fax 703/335-9486, or *careersavvy@impactpublications.com*

Book design and layout by Kristina Ackley

Contents

Contents

Anger and Conflict in the Workplace

1

What Anger Looks Like At Work

Too many people are too angry at work. Workplace violence is an extreme example. Even short of violence, every day you see managers and co-workers who are mad at each other, their co-workers, their employees, their bosses, their customers, the company, and the world itself. Anger interferes with teamwork and productivity. It also creates an environment that is negative, hostile, and frightening. Companies face legal pressures to prevent this type of environment, and from employees' points of view, anger takes the fun out of work. Because anger is a natural emotion, it would be unrealistic to ask people not to feel it. Instead, the goal is to help—and, sometimes, *require*—that at work, they deal with their anger less aggressively and more appropriately.

There are eight familiar *inappropriate* ways both managers and employees deal with anger at work.

Acted-Out Anger

> John didn't like how the meeting was going. He was tired of all these meetings, because they never amounted to anything anyway. It was just a chance for everyone to show off. He'd gone to too many of these meetings, and put up with them for too long. While the discussion went on, he stood up, slammed his copy of the agenda on the table, walked out, and slammed the door behind him.

Acted-Out Anger occurs when managers or employees make it clear they are angry *but* they take no steps to address the problem. They may stomp out of meetings and slam doors, as John did, and they also may yell, scream, throw things, swear, or in many other ways vent their anger. In addition to alienating himself from the team, John also may make his co-workers afraid of him.

If John were to become violent at work, he most likely would do it in ways that are similar to his angry behavior—directly, impulsively, and aimed at whomever was present at the time and whomever he blamed for his problems.

Interestingly, Acted-Out Anger also may take the opposite form:

> Rachel was fed up with the meeting. She was tired of how certain people dominated all the time, and how the others let them get away with it. She was done dealing with any of them. She sat quietly at the meeting, refusing to look at anyone, and refusing to make comments or respond to anyone. Even after the meeting, she avoided saying anything to any of them.

Rachel is pouting. Although her behavior appears calmer and quieter than John's, she is doing the same thing he is—venting her anger, instead of trying to address the cause of it. Her way of venting is different, but the effect is very similar: no one is able to talk to her. Even though no one is likely to fear Rachel, she still has alienated herself from the team.

If Rachel were to become violent at work, she most likely would do it in indirect ways, described in the "Undercover Anger" section below. Although, like John, she vents her anger instead of trying to solve the problem, her form of venting is to withdraw, which means any violence she commits is likely to be less direct than John's.

Both Rachel and John have isolated themselves at work, and both have negatively affected their co-workers. In addition to John and

Rachel losing out, the team, the company, and customers miss out on the talents, skills, and ideas John and Rachel could offer. Their Acted-Out Anger hurts everyone.

Unconnected Anger

Densel didn't know why they kept blaming him. He had a lot of things going on in his life right now, and he couldn't be expected to remember everything. Besides, what did they keep pushing teamwork for, if he was supposed to carry so much of the load himself? Yes, he knew about all the meetings and that each person was supposed to do certain things, but with all his other problems, he had no way to take care of it all. And they should have known.

Now they were saying it was his fault that the project wouldn't get done on time. "Look," he said. "You guys are the ones to blame, not me! I'm handling a lot of things right now and you should have known that. You should have watched my deadlines more closely, and reminded me of everything sooner. Now it's too late. That's your fault!"

Densel takes no responsibility for failing to do his part of the work, and he gets angry when his teammates hold him accountable. Depending on how they react to his Unconnected outburst, the teamwork—and productivity—may fall apart.

If Densel were to become violent at work, he would most likely do so by lashing out against whomever he blamed for his problems. He would feel justified because he experiences problems as coming completely from others and not at all from his own actions. His lack of responsibility makes it easy for him to see himself being victimized.

Day-to-day, Densel alienates himself from his co-workers and hurts his credibility as a good or dependable performer. His Unconnected Anger hurts both the team and himself.

Self-Centered Anger

Maria didn't really care what the reason was for having to wait to take a break. She understood that to make the best use of time, everyone was supposed to wait until the run was finished, so the machine would have to be shut down anyway, to be set up for another product. Her supervisor had explained this enough times to last a lifetime.

"My boyfriend's department takes breaks at the same time every morning," she shouted at her supervisor. "By the time we're ready to shut down this machine, he'll already be back at work. You can't deprive me of seeing him. I'm entitled to a break, and I'm going to take it now."

Even though she knew the reasons for the rules, Maria ignored them when they inconvenienced and angered her. In addition, someone else had to cover for her, so the whole department was affected.

If Maria were to become violent at work, she most likely would do so impulsively, to whomever she perceived as being in her way at the time. She would feel justified because, to her, the only needs or feelings that matter are her own.

Maria's Self-Centered Anger showed that she acts only out of self-interest. Her behavior hurts the team, the company, and her own career.

Undercover Anger

Kelly knew they didn't respect her, and she was tired of being treated like she was less than them. She'd make sure they didn't benefit in any way from her skills or talent. When the mail came, for example, it was her job to distribute it—but that didn't mean she had to put it in the most convenient place for each of them. And just because she was supposed to take messages, that didn't mean she always had to remember to give it to the right person. There were lots of ways she could get even, and they wouldn't even know it. Kelly got a lot of satisfaction just thinking about it.

Kelly undermines her co-workers in two ways: getting even, and not making it clear that she is doing so. The confusion and inconvenience eventually will lead to realization about what Kelly is doing.

If Kelly wanted to hurt someone at work, she would be more likely to commit sabotage—damaging their equipment, for example—than violence against the person, because her way of dealing with anger is indirect and secretive. If she did become violent at work, she most likely would do so in ways that were covert, indirect, and passive, such as failing to tell the person that the handle on their machine was broken and could fly off.

Day-to-day, in addition to hurting the performance of her co-workers, Kelly's Undercover Anger eventually will hurt her own credibility.

Rigid Anger

Russ didn't like to waste time discussing different points of view when he already knew the right way to fix a problem. Gary, one of the managers reporting to him, had called him to this meeting with Gary's staff as they discussed an issue. Everyone had made a few comments, and Russ didn't think they were anywhere near the solution he knew was the best one. Russ knew that Gary wanted his input, and also that Gary wanted to show Russ how well he could work with his team. But all this talk was a waste of time. Gary needed to understand that there were times when a manager should just solve the problem and tell the staff members what to do.

"Before we go any further," Russ interrupted, "I'd like to explain the best way to deal with this issue. I know what will work, so I'm just going to spell it out for you."

In addition to hurting Gary's credibility in the eyes of Gary's staff, Russ undermined the team process and the buy-in and other benefits that come with it. Russ is more interested in having his way than in listening, learning, or giving others a chance for input.

If Russ were to become violent at work, he would likely do so in ways that were pre-planned and to the person(s) he blamed for preventing him from being in control. The greater his need for control, the greater the risk that losing control—or perceiving that he is losing control—could cause him to overreact.

Russ's need for control makes it easy for him to get angry when he cannot make others do what he wants. His Rigid Anger hurts the team, the company, and his own reputation

Escapist Anger

Justin was fed up with the way they picked on him. His manager and HR rep kept ganging up on him, accusing him of forgetting to take care of certain things, coming in late most of the time, and arguing with his supervisor a lot. He'd done a pretty good job of making up good reasons for the problems, but they never seemed to buy it. Now that he'd missed three more days of work, he knew they'd really get on him.

They told him to go to his manager's office. Well, he would, and when he saw her, he'd tell her off for picking on him. He was annoyed to find the HR rep there.

"We have a problem," his manager said. "Your performance and attendance keep getting worse. We've made arrangements to have you go take a drug test right now. You have to take the test before you can return to work."

"You're both against me," Justin shouted. "I'll file an EEO complaint! I'll have you both fired! I'm a good worker and you've both falsified my records."

Justin's denial only increases the negative impact of his Escapist Anger. He feels picked on and angry, even though he clearly has a history of problems regarding attendance and performance—and regarding telling the truth.

If Justin were to become violent at work, he most likely would target whomever exposed his lies. The truth would shatter the life he had created with elaborate lies and justifications, and he would feel exposed and trapped. There also is the possibility that he would be under the influence of drugs, alcohol, or other substances that affected his judgment.

In his everyday work, Justin's Escapist Anger makes his co-workers and supervisor unable to count on him, anticipate his mood, or believe him.

Shocking Anger

Yung-Su didn't speak up much at meetings, but she had good working relationships with her co-workers and her manager. A hard worker with lots of good idea, she had a reputation for being a good performer and easy to get along with. That's why everyone was shocked at Yung-Su's reaction when her manager told her she would not get the promotion she'd hoped for.

Yung-Su stood up, leaned towards the manager, and in a voice loud enough for everyone to hear, said, "You'll be very sorry."

Although Yung-Su's behavior could fit under the Acted-Out Anger heading, the key is that what she did was very much out of character for her.

If Yung-Su were to become violent at work, she most likely would do so impulsively. Of the eight categories of inappropriate expressions of anger, hers is the most likely to surprise co-workers and managers because her usual behavior is so unlike her angry outbursts.

In everyday interactions, the contrast between Yung-Su's general behavior and her Shocking Anger creates doubts in other's minds, and makes her seem unpredictable to them.

Strange Anger

Charlie never related very well to anyone at work. He almost never made eye contact with anyone, and if he did, he looked away very quickly. Charlie barely responded when anything was said to him. He carried out his duties as a janitor pretty well, but occasionally there were rumors that he talked to himself and made unusual facial expressions.

One day when Charlie couldn't find a water leak, he got angry and started yelling at the pipes. "My enemies changed your DNA," he shouted at the pipes. "They did it to set me up!"

This type of anger is difficult to address, because the person experiencing it is not dealing with the same reality with which most of us are familiar. This expression of anger is confusing, and it can create misunderstanding, uncertainty, and fear within the organization.

If Charlie were to become violent, it very likely would be in ways that are bizarre and extreme. A familiar example is the Unabomber's letter-bombs.

Day-to-day, Charlie's Strange Anger makes co-workers and managers afraid of him.

All Eight Anger Types—and Conflict

These eight ways of dealing with anger are inappropriate because they hurt the team, the company, the customers, and also the employees and managers who exhibit them. To make it worse, individuals often exhibit more than one of these types of anger.

When individuals demonstrate anger in these ways, they usually end up in conflict with others. The conflicts are rarely resolved in any real ways, because true resolution takes cooperation, patience, and specific skills. Unfortunately, the forcefulness, underhandedness, or persistence of employees and managers demonstrating these eight types of anger usually evoke, in others, a desire to appease in order to get the conflict over with. Too often, the short-term "solutions" consist of the following:

Type of Anger	**Short-term (Ineffective) "Solutions"**
Acted-Out Anger:	Fear, avoidance, staying out of their way
Unconnected Anger:	Accepting their blame, finishing their work for them, and resenting them for it
Self-Centered Anger:	Filling-in for them and resenting them for it
Undercover Anger:	Going undercover oneself by talking "behind their backs" about what they are doing
Rigid Anger:	Giving in, feeling intimidated, and resenting them for it

Escapist Anger:	Believing them, making up for their mistakes, questioning oneself, covering for them
Shocking Anger:	"Explaining it away," making up reasons for why the person acted in such unlikely ways, and dismissing it
Strange Anger:	Fear, avoidance, failure to do anything

None of these reactions help anyone. Instead, these reactions allow the anger, the performance problems, and the negative relationships to continue—and to worsen. All eight inappropriate expressions of anger, on the part of individuals, lead to conflicts within the entire team or company. Companies face legal risks because of the hostile atmosphere. Individual employees and managers face a work environment that is, at best, less fun, less creative, and less productive than it could be—and, at worst, is a hostile and perhaps even dangerous place.

The fact that people act these ways does *not* mean they'll become violent. It *does* mean they deal poorly with their anger, and they create a workplace that is, at best, angry. The goal is to lower this anger long before it escalates, to create a workplace that is more fun—and more productive.

Because anger is natural and real, the way to create a better and more productive workplace is to replace the eight inappropriate ways of dealing with anger with ways that work.

Although you can't change everyone in your organization by yourself, this book will show you how you *can* manage your own anger, the conflicts you get into, and the anger and conflicts around you. By dealing well with your own anger and conflicts, you can influence everyone around you and help make your workplace less angry. You will acquire skills for successfully managing anger and conflict in the workplace.

These skills are based on thousands of hours I've spent consulting in corporations and talking with individuals who were angry at work. The skills worked for them. They will work for you—*and* your workplace.

Assess Your Workplace

Here's a quick quiz to take, to find out just *how* angry *your* workplace is. Check every statement that applies to where you work:

_____ Employees/managers pout, yell, scream, throw things or, in other ways, make it clear that they are angry. (Acted-Out Anger)

_____ When they are held accountable for something, employees/managers express their anger by blaming others for their own mistakes. (Unconnected Anger)

_____ Employees/managers get angry when they cannot have things their way. (Self-Centered Anger)

_____ Employees/managers hold grudges, are resentful, or find ways to get even with others. (Undercover Anger)

_____ Employees/managers get angry when they are not in control of the situation or of others. (Rigid Anger)

_____ Employees/managers lie or use drugs or alcohol, and get angry when they are caught at either. (Escapist Anger)

_____ Employees/managers express their anger in ways that are extreme or out of character. (Shocking Anger)

_____ Employees/managers are extremely remote or withdrawn, and deal with their anger in bizarre ways. (Strange Anger)

Anger is natural. Problems don't come from anger—problems come from the *negative ways* people *express* anger.

2

Anger Is a Behavior that Can Be Managed

Although you cannot fix all the anger problems where you work, you *can* do three things:

- You can change your own way of dealing with *your* anger.
- You can change your reactions to your co-workers', employees', and manager's anger.
- Through your new behaviors, you can *influence* the way your co-workers, employees, and manager deal with *their* anger.

The first place to start is to recognize what makes people act the way they do, and see how individuals' behaviors influence each other.

Over the years, researchers have developed three main answers to the question, "Why do people act they way they do?"

The first answer looks like this:

ANSWER #1: Attitude ——> Behavior

According to Answer #1, what a person thinks or believes (attitude) leads directly to what he or she does (behavior). Answer #1 says that attitude leads to behavior.

Here is an example of how behavioral problems were treated in the days when Answer #1 appeared to tell the whole story. Joe was an alcoholic. Based on Answer #1, Joe's problem looked like this:

Joe's attitude ——> Joe's drinking

Because Joe's drinking appeared to be the result of his attitude, everyone worked very hard to change Joe's attitude:

- They explained to Joe *why* he drank: family problems, poor upbringing, stress, and other reasons.
- Then they explained to Joe *why* he should quit drinking: health risks, job problems, relationship problems.

And if Answer #1 were correct, the situation would have changed this way:

Joe's new attitude ——> Joe quits drinking

Unfortunately, this almost never happened. Instead, the result looked more like this:

Joe's new understanding ——> Justification for his drinking

Joe continued to drink, and felt justified because of all the bad things that had happened to him.

Even though Answer #1 may have explained part of why people act the way they do, it left some things out. Researchers later came up with the second answer, which looked like this:

ANSWER #2: Attitude <——> Behavior

In Answer #2, attitude and behavior influence each other. This means that while attitude very well may influence Joe's behavior, his behavior also influences his attitude. Using Answer #2, everyone decided to forget trying to change Joe's attitude. Instead, they focused on his *behavior*, by putting him in a room with very soft walls and no alcohol. This time, the change in Joe's behavior came *before* the change in his attitude: he quit drinking long before he decided to. Other behaviors, such as talking one-on-one with a counselor and talking in groups with fellow alcoholics, gave Joe support for this change. And here's what happened to Joe. After a period of time of not drinking (maybe two or three months of total abstinence), Joe *decided* to quit drinking. His new attitude came *after* his behavior. It looked like Answer #2 said it all.

Unfortunately, therapists and counselors did not realize that something important still was missing. Even after Joe stopped drinking and decided against drinking, he still was at risk. If he left the clinic and returned to his alcoholic friends, it was merely a matter of time before Joe would begin to drink again. What therapists had overlooked was the environment—the other people in Joe's life.

Today, the third answer to why people act the way they do looks like this Behavior Wheel:

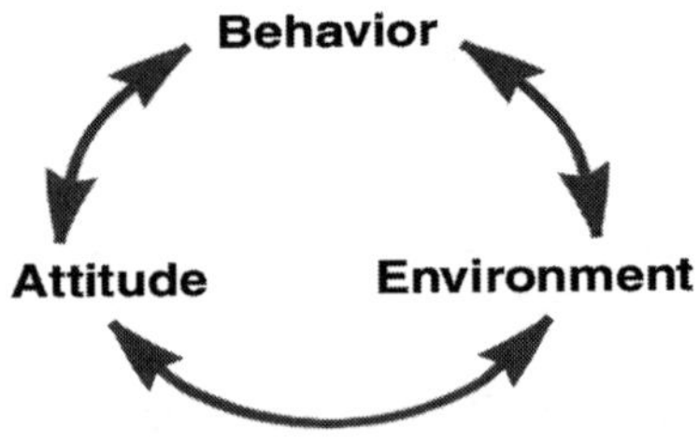

Because the arrows go both directions, Answer #3 says that what we think, how we act, and how others respond to us all affect each other equally. Each can cause any of the others, and each can be an effect of the others. For Joe, the Behavior Wheel looks like this:

According to this answer, the way to stop Joe's drinking—and keep it stopped is to get him to quit (change his behavior), allow time for his new behavior to influence his decisions (behavior change affects his attitudes), and have him find friends who do not drink (environment supports his new behavior).

Answer #3, or the Behavior Wheel, is based on A. Bandura's *Social Learning Theory* (Prentice-Hall, 1977). The Behavior Wheel says we act the way we do because of the *interaction* among our behavior, our environment, and our attitudes.

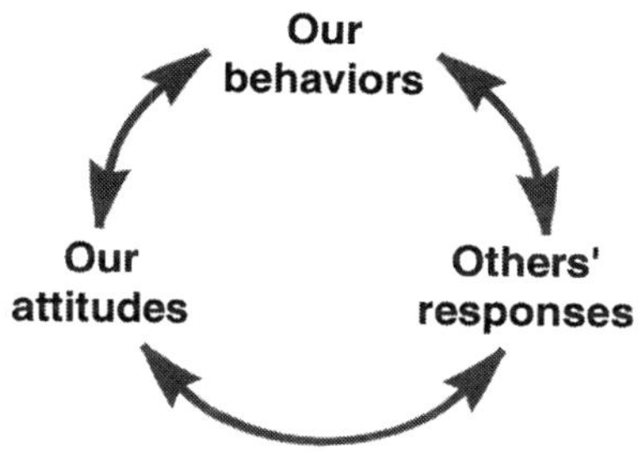

The Behavior Wheel also says several powerful things:

- As in Answer #2, our behavior can affect our attitudes. Sometimes it is easier and faster to change our behavior than to change our ideas, beliefs or feelings. Joe quit drinking before he decided to.
- How other people respond to us influences how we feel. But our feelings about ourselves also affect how others re-

spond to us. If Joe feels down and vulnerable, his drinking buddies are more likely to encourage him to drink. If he feels content and secure, they are more likely to leave the decision up to him.

- The responses from others responses affect our behavior, but our actions also can influence their responses. Just as others can tempt Joe to drink again, Joe's refusal to drink can influence his friends. They either will quit tempting him, quit drinking themselves, or end their friendship with Joe (in which case his behavior will attract new friends who do not drink).
- Sometimes, we have to change our environment to support our new behavior. In Joe's case, as with many recovering substance abusers, he may have to change friends to stay away from alcohol.

Of these three elements, the easiest to change is our own behavior. Once our behavior changes, so do our own attitudes. And, so do the responses we attract from others.

This cycle truly portrays a self-fulfilling prophecy. It shows how our expectations, whether positive or negative, come true through the interaction among our attitudes, our behaviors and the responses of others in the environment. In Joe's case, the Behavior Wheel looks like this:

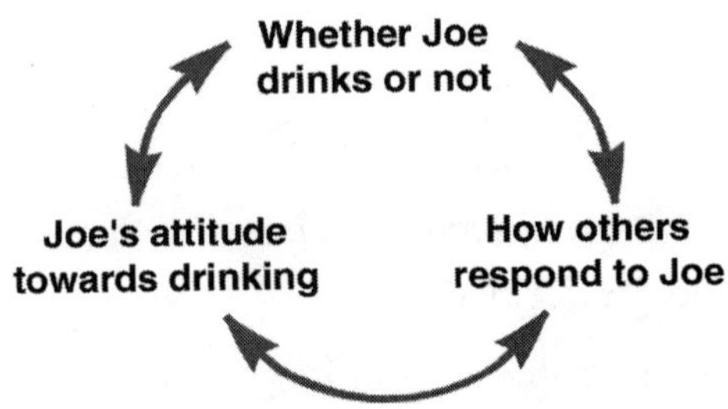

Using the same ideas regarding anger, we can describe the interaction this way:

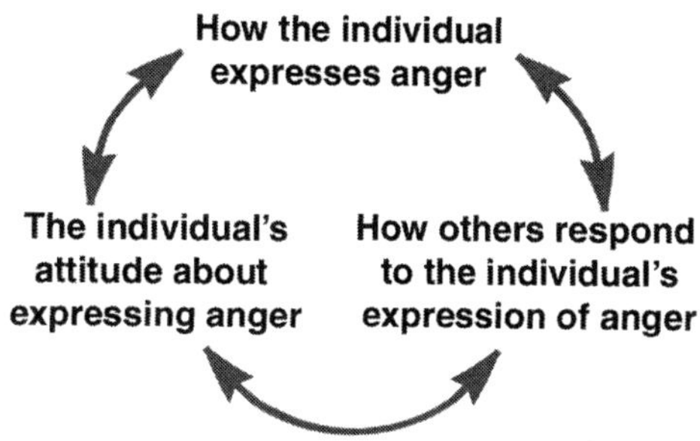

Changes can occur in several ways:

- If you change the way you express your anger, you can get different reactions from others at work, and you also can change your attitude about how you should express anger.
- If you change your attitudes, beliefs, and ideas about how you express your anger, you can change how you behave when you're angry, and how your co-workers, employees, and managers respond to you.
- Depending on how you feel about the responses you get, the ways your co-workers, employees, and managers respond when you are angry can change your behaviors and your attitudes.
- Your own responses to others' expressions of anger can influence their behaviors and attitudes.

Chapter 1 identified ineffective responses to each of the eight inappropriate expressions of anger. Here are examples of how responses can influence behavior. Remember that you, alone, cannot change others' behaviors at work. However, you can be a contributor and a role-model for others who also can respond in ways that contribute to change.

Acted-Out Anger

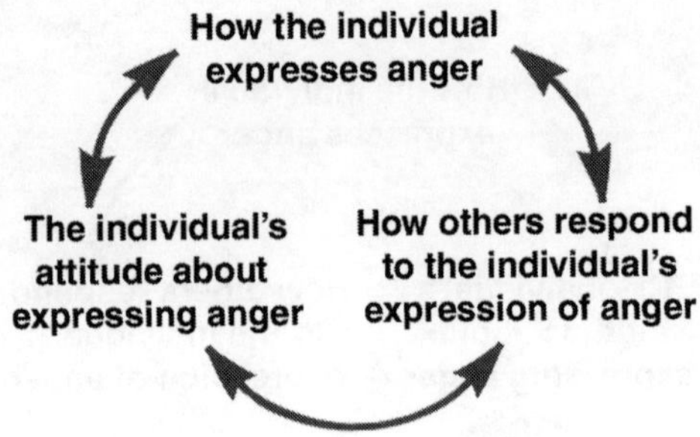

When the responses to Acted-Out Anger are fear, avoidance, and staying out of their way, these angry individuals get what they want: reinforcement of the belief that they have victimized others. As a result, they will continue to carry out their Acted-Out Anger behaviors.

If you respond in ways that do *not* reinforce this belief, you may be able to contribute to a change in their behavior. There are many options, described later on, but one example may be to make a factual statement (such as, "Your behavior is not appropriate here at work.") and walk away. If the behavior is extreme enough, another response might be to call the police. The point is that instead of victimizing others, the individuals using Acted-Out Anger feel less powerful and, perhaps, even foolish. Their Behavior Wheel will look like this:

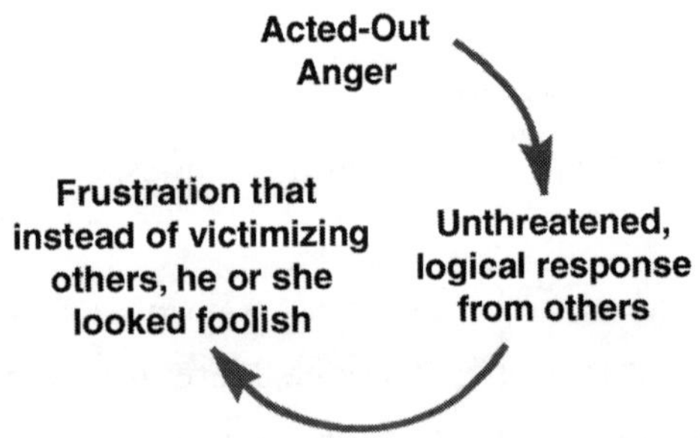

These unexpected responses can help lead to changes in their behaviors and attitudes.

Unconnected Anger

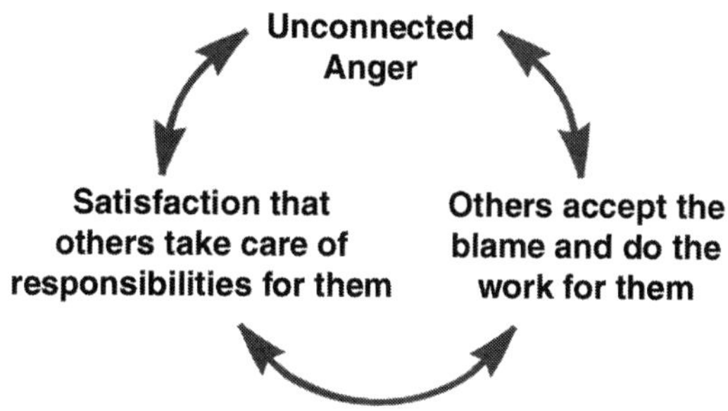

In this case, the individuals who show Unconnected Anger get reinforcement that they really are *not* to blame, that they have no responsibilities, and that others should take care of their work. To counteract this reinforcement, an effective response might be to let the responsibilities remain unfinished and let the consequences fall on those who failed to do what they should. Their Behavior Wheel will look like this:

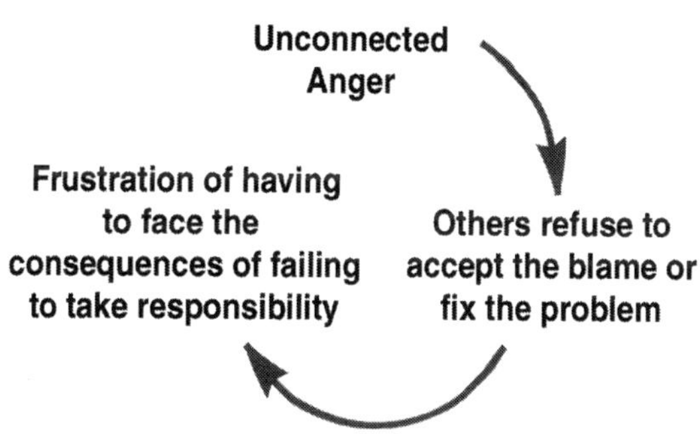

Individuals demonstrating Unconnected Anger will learn—in a hurry—that they can't get away with blaming others or failing to take ownership when they should.

In the short run, these responses may cause problems at work. However, they will make glaringly obvious what—and who—was responsible for the original problem. If you choose to respond this way, it may help to make sure, in advance, that your manager understands and supports what you plan to do. Your "selling point" is that in the long run, this type of response can eliminate problems related to Unconnected Anger.

Self-Centered Anger

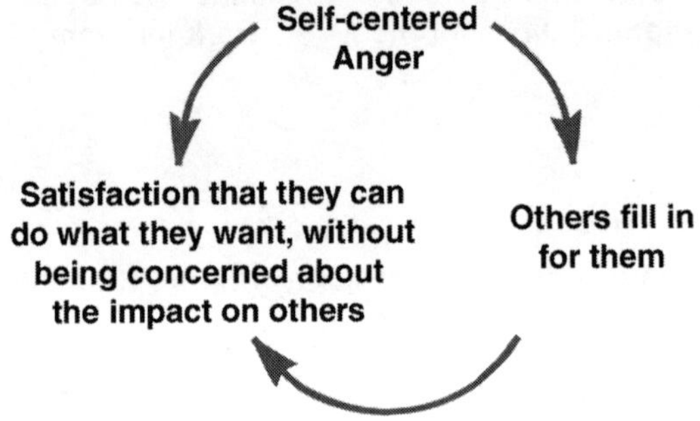

When others fill in for individuals who exhibit Self-Centered Anger, these responses show the individuals that they can do as they please without having to consider the impact on their co-workers, employees, managers, the company, or customers. An example of a response that could contribute to changes in their behavior would be to refuse to cover for them and let the outcomes and consequences fall as they may. Another would be to hold them accountable—and require them to make up for the time they lost, or to repair the damages caused by their Self-Centered Anger. Their new Behavior Wheel will look like this:

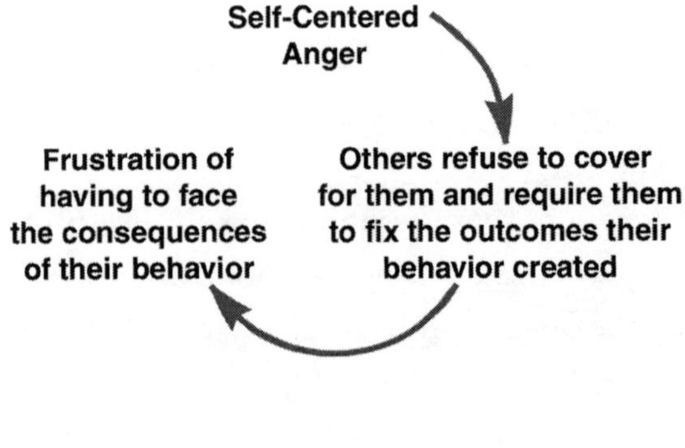

Having to deal with the consequences of their own actions will be harder for them than if they had considered their impact on others in the first place. Experience—brought about by others' responses—is likely to motivate them to change their Self-Centered Anger.

Undercover Anger

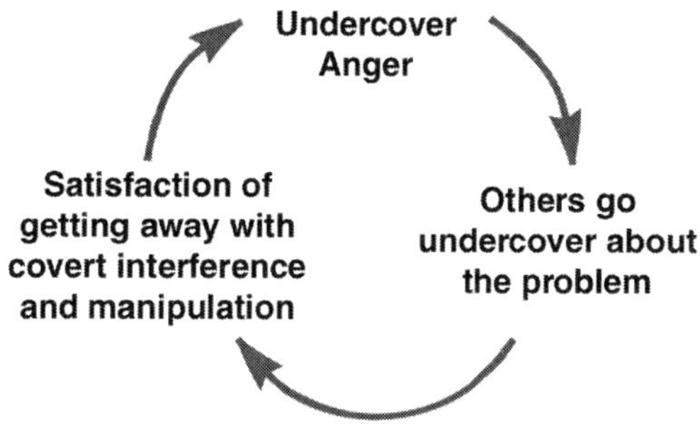

When others go undercover by complaining "behind the backs" of individuals who display Undercover Anger, these individuals "win" because they got everyone else to act like them. To counter Undercover Anger, one response may be to bring the problem out into the open. For example, if a co-worker exhibits Undercover Anger, others may give specific examples (such as not giving messages to the right people) to the manager and include the fact that the covert nature of these behaviors adds to the problem. Their new Behavior Wheel will look like this:

In addition to having their covert tactics exposed, individuals exhibiting Undercover Anger also will suffer public knowledge that their actions also are performance issues. Both facts can be motivators for changes in their Undercover Anger.

Rigid Anger

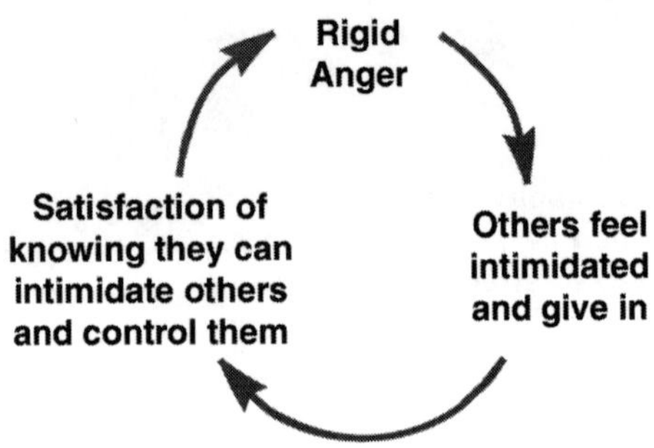

When individuals who demonstrate Rigid Anger get their way because others feel intimidated, the power-seekers' desire to control others gets reinforced—and tends to increase. It is difficult to counter these individuals, because of the nature of intimidation. But an effective response that could help change their behavior would be to address the intimidation itself. For example, saying "I know you are making a point about this topic, but the way you're talking is too forceful and intimidating to allow for any real discussion" would get to the heart of the issue. Bringing the intimidation out in the open—in a calm, straightforward manner—would lower its impact. Their new Behavior Wheel will look like this:

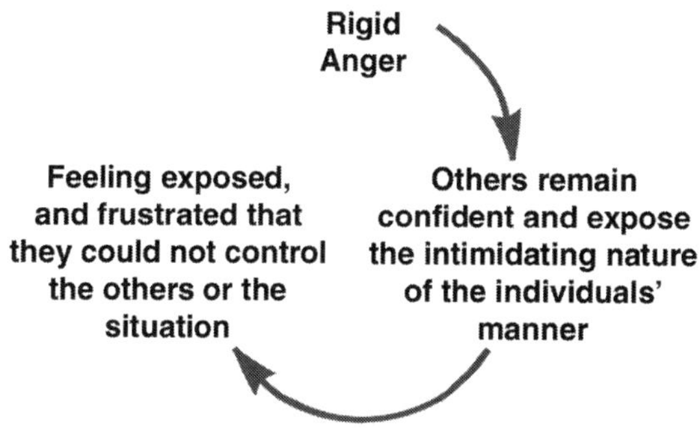

The changes in response can result in fewer attempts to control or intimidate others. They also can result in more genuine, and effective, discussions and decision-making.

Escapist Anger

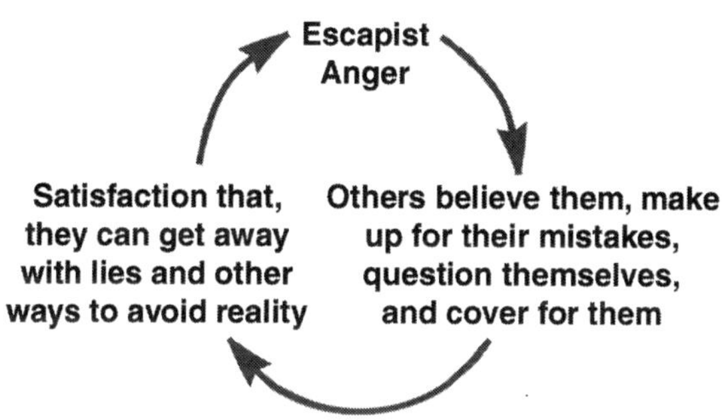

Without intending to, others reinforce the illusions and fabrications constructed by the individuals who display Escapist Anger. Others' actions allow these individuals to avoid the consequences of their behavior and believe their own lies. When others question their own memories or judgment, these individuals have "won" by getting others unwittingly to avoid reality.

Responses that can change Escapist Anger have to bring reality to the forefront. For example, refusing to cover for them and making them deal with their own consequences will "bring reality home." Recognizing their lies for what they are—and calling them on it—is another example. It's also important to trust your own awareness of what is real and what is not. Their new Behavior Wheel will be:

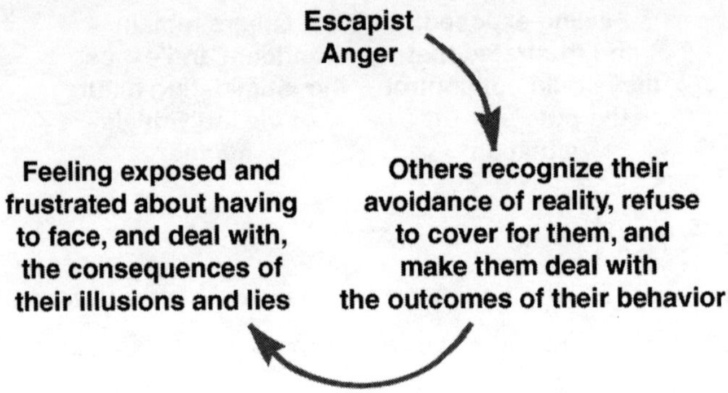

The changes in others' responses can have a powerful effect on individuals who demonstrate Escapist Anger. Much like the examples earlier of Joe, the alcoholic, these individuals' entire approach to life is being challenged. Although the process can be difficult, the long-term results will be worth it—for everyone else at work, as well as for these individuals.

Shocking Anger

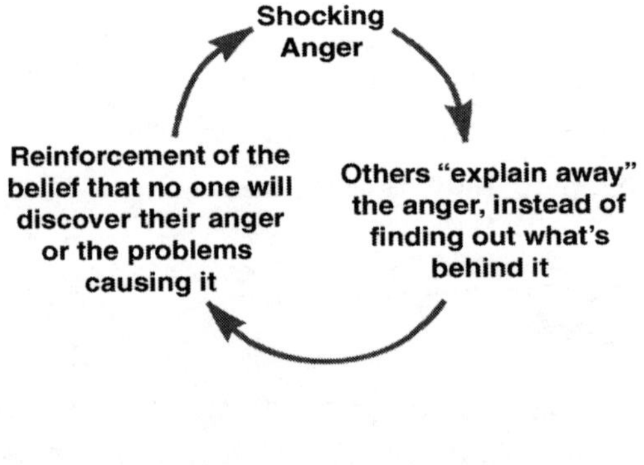

When others dismiss the Shocking Anger because it's "out of character" for the individuals exhibiting it, the anger—and the problems behind it—never get addressed. The risk is that the anger will continue to surface unexpectedly, and perhaps in dangerous ways. Sometimes, this means that the individuals displaying Shocking Anger get to keep their anger a "secret," which means they get away with sporadic outbursts of it. At the same time, however, it also might mean that someone who needs help is not able to get it, because co-workers, employees, and managers do not recognize the Shocking Anger as a plea for help. When problems are not recognized, they cannot be addressed.

Different responses could bring the problems out in the open, where they can be resolved. The simplest change would be to make a point of the fact that the Shocker Anger *is* out of character, and that because it is, there is all the more reason to find out what's behind it. In this case, the Behavior Wheel would look like this:

At the very least, the change in others' responses will reveal problems that others, or the company, need to have addressed. At the very best, individuals who need help will get the attention and help they need.

Strange Anger

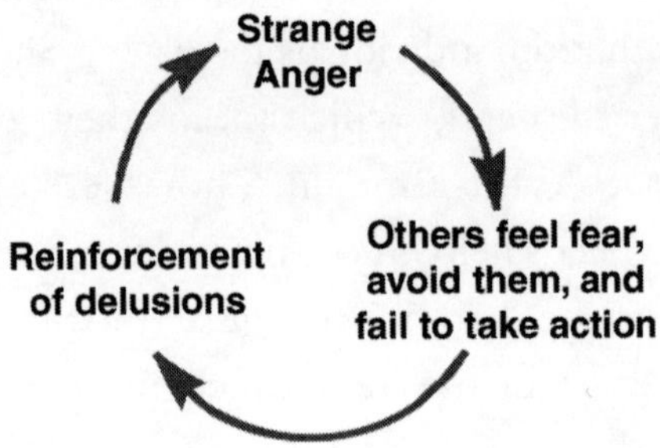

When others fail to act in the face of Strange Anger, they reinforce the delusions—some of which may be paranoid—of the individuals exhibiting these behaviors. The risk is that without getting the help they need, these individuals can be harmful to others as well as to themselves.

The fear others feel often comes from two sources: the Strange Anger, and the individuals' history of poor—sometimes very unusual—social skills. To help change the behavior of individuals exhibiting Strange Anger, others do not have to put themselves in risky situations. For example, they can respond to Strange Anger by offering help rather than by disciplining. Instead of saying, "I'm going to write you up (or report you to your boss) for this behavior," it would be more effective to say, "It looks like you need a chance to talk to someone, so I'll get HR (or your manager, or the Employee Assistance person)." The new Behavior Wheel will look like:

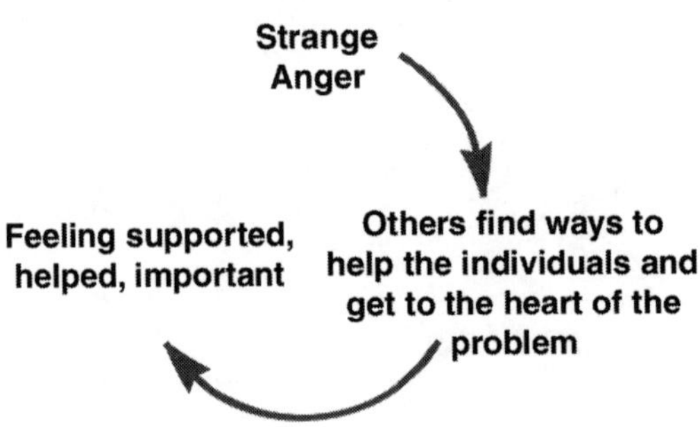

Everyone—including those exhibiting Strange Anger—benefits from these changes in others' responses.

In all these examples, you can be in either position: the person exhibiting the inappropriate expression of anger, or the person responding to this behavior. You can't "fix" everyone, but you can manage your own Behavior Wheel and you can play an active, positive role in others' Behavior Wheels.

Now you are ready for specific skills that will help you manage your own behavior when you are angry and will help you react to others' anger in ways that can influence them for the better.

3

The First Skill: Deciding

Before you can use specific skills for managing anger, you must first ask yourself three questions:

1. **Do you want to work things out with the other person?** It's easy to assume that "everyone" wants to work things out. But even if you want to in principle, you may not feel that way at the moment. If you are the angry one and are really into your anger, you may not feel like working things out just then. You would be better off waiting until you calm down. If you are the target of the angry person, you may feel too protective or defensive at the moment, and again would benefit from waiting. These skills will work only if—and when—you are ready to want them to.

2. **Does the other person want to work things out with you?** Although we like to assume that they do, it's possible that they, too, are too emotional at the moment to want to work on it. They also may have hidden agendas that keep them at odds with you. For example, someone who exhibits Undercover Anger may want to "get even" with you by making you look bad, and therefore would benefit if it appears that that you "can't get along with others." Whether

it's for temporary emotional reasons, or for long-term personal or political reasons, others may not want to work things out with you. In these cases, the skills will not work, because the other person's goal is to keep the anger or conflict going. These skills will work only if—and when—*both* of you want them to.

Interestingly, if the other person does *not* want to work it out with you, the skills will *not* work. In this case, you have only two options: ignore the individual, or get someone with authority to back you. Ignoring them usually is difficult at work, because you have to work with them to do your job and you don't want it to be evident that you're having trouble with someone at work. To gain the other person's cooperation and willingness to do his or her part of the work, you may have to get your manager's help.

Co-workers, employees, and managers who exhibit any of the eight inappropriate types of anger are likely to appear, at first, as if they do *not* want to work things out with you. And in many situations, this will be true. However, the skills described in this book can build on even the smallest shred of willingness the other person may have. It helps to stay open to the possibility that they will work with you on this, and use the skills to increase the likelihood. It also helps if you can start out assuming they want to cooperate and they just need some help using the skills that make it possible. If these efforts lead nowhere, it's time to get your manager's help.

3. **If you are a "bystander," and not the angry person or the target of the angry person, is it appropriate for you to get involved?** A lot depends on your role and relationship with them. If, for example, you are their manager,

> it would be appropriate to get involved if they could not work things out or if their anger disrupted the workplace. If you are a co-worker, or a manager without authority over these individuals, it may or may not be appropriate for you to get involved. Several of the skills will help you recognize differences between roles and will help you determine whether, when, and how to become involved.

Once you've answered these questions, determined that both you and the other person want to work things out, and decided that it was appropriate for you to do something, you are ready to use six more skills to manage anger. These skills are covered in the following chapters. You'll see how to use them whether you are the one who's angry, you are the one the other person is angry at, or you are the bystander.

You are likely to use only a few of these skills at any one time, and except for the first one—Deciding—they do not work in any particular order. You can think of these skills as tools that serve different purposes, and the "right" tools will depend on each situation.

4

The Second Skill: Be Direct

Too often, anger at work comes from not being able to say what you mean to the right person. We don't know who has the authority to take the action we want done, or we know who it is but do not have access to them, or we do have access but they don't want to hear what we have to say, or it's not "politically correct" to say what we want to say, or we're so frustrated that we tell everyone around us instead of those who could do something. We see things at work that should be changed, but we can't make that happen because we don't have the authority and we can't get through to those who do—and our anger builds.

Tony was tired of hearing it. Every day, the boss complained about the number of rejects, and every day Tony and the rest of the team told him that the equipment was at fault. It was old and couldn't meet the specs with any regularity, and it had to be replaced with newer technology. The boss should have figured this out by now, but nothing's changed. Worse, Tony knew that at performance-review time, they'd all get blamed even though everyone on the crew knew what the real problem was.

Tony got angry just thinking about it. The very sight of the equipment made him angry, and the sight of the boss was starting to fill him with rage.

Tony's frustration is familiar. His Behavior Wheel looks like this:

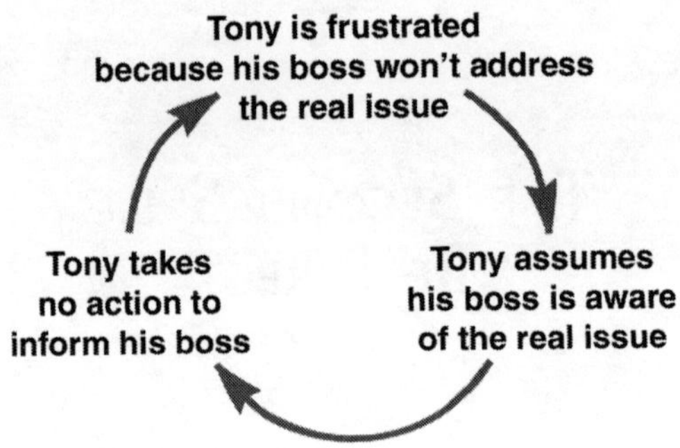

Despite the fact that he's so frustrated, his own assumptions are preventing him from taking steps that could solve the problem. Tony needs a way to get past his own assumptions and *make sure* his manager knows what the real issue is. He also needs to do this in a way that will show he is a professional who is committed to solving the problem, rather than a complainer, whiner, or blamer.

Skill Two: Be Direct

Being direct does *not* mean being blunt, barging in on the boss, or coming across forcefully. It means:

- Going to the right person (instead of talking to everyone else about it)
- Making clear what your goals or purposes are
- Being specific about what your "real issues" are

Here is an example of how Tony could use this skill with his manager:

Going to the right person:

- Tony will go to his manager.

Tony's goals and purposes:

- Improve productivity (through greater accuracy and more efficiency)
- Enable the team to feel proud of their performance (instead of frustrated)

Tony's real issues:

- The old equipment—*not* the workers—are the cause of low productivity
- The equipment should be replaced with newer technology

Letting go:

- Tony does not have the authority to make changes. His manager does.
- Once Tony tells his manager what Tony sees as the real issues, Tony has done all he can.

Based on these points, Tony can approach his manager this way:

"I'd like to talk to you about improving productivity in our department," Tony said, "and also about helping the workers feel proud of their work."

"Yes," the manager said, "anything that improves productivity will make us *all* happy! What have you got in mind?"

"Well, so far, the workers have been blamed for the low productivity," Tony said. "But the real cause is the equipment. It's old, it's slow, and it can't meet the specs. We need newer technology."

Tony has taken all three steps in being direct:

- going to his manager
- specifying his goals
- specifying his real issues.

Tony cannot be sure how his manager will react, because the manager's reactions are outside Tony's control. However, Tony will no longer feel angry, because he took action that *could* lead to solutions. Now, Tony's Behavior Wheel looks like this:

Notice the emphasis on the fact that Tony's actions *could* lead to solutions and his manager *may* get new equipment—and that Tony's anger will leave even though he doesn't know, and cannot control, the outcome.

The last step of being direct, "Letting Go," means Tony recognizes that telling his manager about the real issues is all that he has the authority to do.

When it comes to managing anger at work, the skill of *being direct* gives us a chance to do the one thing we *can* control—take action that is within our area of responsibility. Tony's anger dissipates because Tony has done all he could. Now the rest is up to his manager.

When You Don't Get the Solutions You Want

Tony's actions took care of the first source of his anger—his manager's failure to understand the real issues. But the anger may return again if the second source of Tony's anger doesn't change—his manager's failure to take the action Tony wants him to take.

In this situation, we have to look further into the "Letting Go" part of being direct. Tony's anger has several "layers" or levels, all of which are real:

- The first, most obvious and most primitive, level is that Tony did not get what he wanted.
- The second, most immediate, level is that his manager did not replace the equipment.
- On the third level down, Tony is angry because he doesn't have the authority to do what he thinks is necessary, even though he knows more than his boss knows about it.
- On the fourth level down, Tony's anger is that he (and all the workers) will continue to get blamed for low productivity even though it's not their fault.
- On the fifth level down, Tony is angry at the unfairness of the whole situation at work, all the managers, and the company overall.
- On the sixth level down, Tony's anger from *other* unfair situations going on in his life add to his anger about the work problem.
- On the seventh level down, Tony's anger from other unfair situations he's gone through in the past add to his anger about the work problem.
- On the eighth level, Tony's anger applies to everyone and Tony sees the whole world as unfair to him.

Anger that is not dealt with appropriately can accumulate this way and can affect the way we see events going on in the present. If Tony's not careful, his anger will intensify until others wonder why he is *so* angry about his manager's failure to replace the equipment. Others can relate to the first two levels of Tony's anger, but they don't understand about levels three through eight.

Interestingly, Tony may not be aware of these levels either. He will feel the anger without recognizing how many sources it comes from. And he'll feel justified thinking it's all about his manager's failure to get new equipment. Tony's intense anger—which others may see as an "overreaction"—can get out of hand quickly. That's why it's important to understand more about the "Letting Go" step.

Letting go means that:

- We have to accept the fact that we can't always have our way.
- We have to acknowledge, to ourselves, that even though we "know" this, we still don't like it.
- Once we've taken those actions that are within our range of authority, we have to look for ways to work with, deal with, or put up with what's there. For example, if Tony's manager doesn't replace the equipment, Tony has several choices about the letting-go step:
    - He can remind himself that he can't always have things his way.
    - He can acknowledge, to himself, that it's too bad because his ideas are really good.
    - He can "work with" the reality by finding ways to make the old equipment work better.
    - He can "deal with" the reality by transferring to another department, or by documenting his efforts as a way of "covering his tracks."

- He can "put up with" the reality by doing the best he can and *depersonalizing* the department's failure to improve productivity.

The purpose of letting go is to prevent the anger from rising and to feel the satisfaction of having done all you can—despite the fact that what you can do may seem small.

Being direct helps you make the most of doing what you can.

5

The Third Skill: Acknowledge Feelings

When we say that angry people "lose it," we're more accurate than we think. Anger can be so intense that for the moment, we "lose" our calm demeanor, our logical processes, and our future-orientation. Anger can, for a while, dominate everything else we know.

Yet, ironically, most people's typical reaction to angry individuals is to "explain" to them the situation that caused the anger—as if the information can make the anger go away. For example:

> Dustin's face was red. He was tired of putting in so many hours, and now at this meeting they were saying how the schedule would stay the same "for a while." He'd had enough. He got up and walked out of the room, slamming the door behind him.
>
> Jorge, one of the managers, followed Dustin. In the hall, he said, "Look, Dustin, calm down. We have to do this because we can't find enough qualified workers right now, and—"
>
> Dustin glared at him, turned, and walked away.

Even though Jorge meant well, he made the same mistake most of us make—thinking that explanations will remove the anger. Although we do not intend it as such, what "explanations" *really* do is:

- deny the other person's anger
- compete with their anger for attention
- change the focus from *what they are feeling* to *why you think they shouldn't feel that way*

All three of these results deny the angry individuals' experience—which is why they usually react with increased anger or even rage. The Behavior Wheel looks like this:

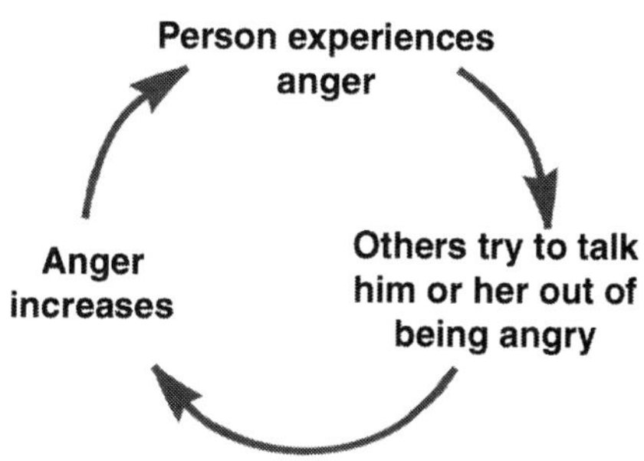

Skill Three: Acknowledge Feelings

Instead of trying to "explain away" their anger, you'll have an easier time if you acknowledge the anger, talk about it, listen to the person experiencing it, and validate it—before you try to talk about the facts or other issues. The angry person can be calmer and more reasonable if he or she first has a chance to be heard. Jorge would have had more success if he'd said something that allowed Dustin to vent verbally. For example, Jorge could have said:

- "It looks like you're angry about the schedule."
- "It doesn't seem fair, does it?"
- "You're entitled to feel the way you do."

Any of these—or similar—comments would allow Dustin to vent. He might say:

- "You bet I'm angry. I'm tired of working so many hours!"
- "No, it's not fair at all. It's too much work when there are so few of us."
- "I sure am entitled to feel this way! I've been working so many hours I can't stand it!"

In all three cases, Dustin would be able to vent and to feel heard. Interestingly, at the same time, his responses would allow for some agreement between him and Jorge—not necessarily about the work schedule, but about *how Dustin feels.* This agreement about Dustin's feelings, and the opportunity for Dustin to vent and be heard, would pave the way for further discussion about the issue at hand—the work schedule. In this example, the Behavior Wheel is:

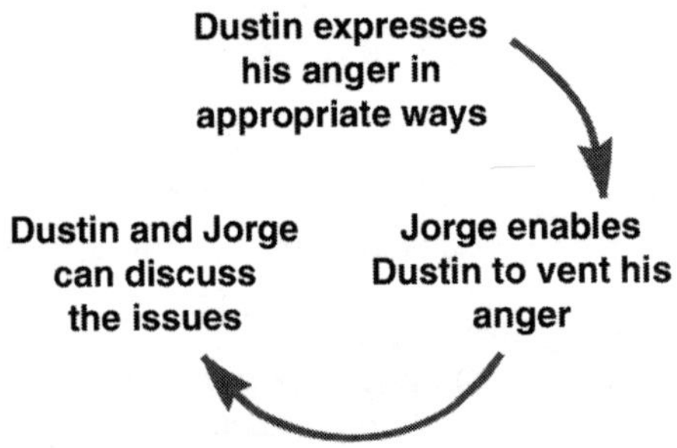

When the other person is angry, the third skill is to acknowledge his or her feelings. If you are genuine, the explanations, discussions, and perhaps even the solutions can follow.

If *you* are the angry person, you can help others, and yourself, by acknowledging to them how you feel.

Erin was upset about the things going on at home. She tried to keep it separate from her work, but she also knew that others probably could tell something was bothering her. She didn't want them to think it was anything or anyone at work.

When Jen and Al walked in, Erin told them, "I just want you both to know that if I'm not in my usual good mood today, it has nothing to do with either of you or with anyone at work."

Both Jen and Al nodded their heads. "Thanks," each said.

By acknowledging her feelings—to herself, and then to her co-workers—Erin avoided misperceptions others may have had about her anger. At the same time, being able to acknowledge the anger also allowed the anger to dissipate.

Erin's Behavior Wheel looks like this:

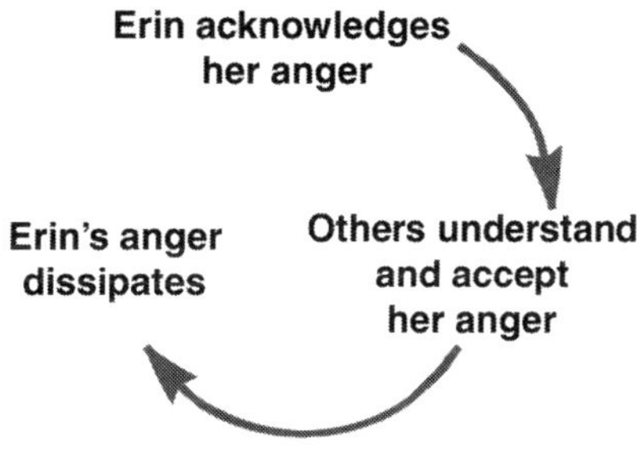

Even if Erin's anger had been directed at Jen or Al, she still could acknowledge it and then, when both she and Jen or Al were ready, they could discuss it and resolve the issues. For example:

Erin told Jen, "I feel angry because something you said at the meeting today made it sound as if I hadn't taken care of the work I was responsible for. I'd like to talk this over when you're ready."

"I understand," Jen said. "How about getting together at 3 today?"

Erin is able to acknowledge her anger without acting angry, and Jen is able to hear about it without getting defensive. Their Behavior Wheel looks like this:

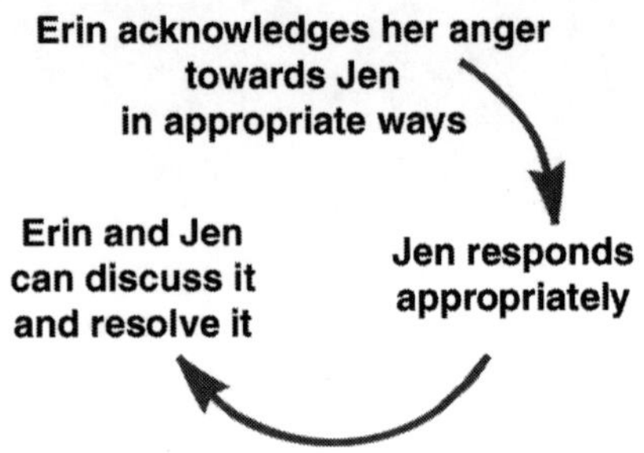

When you are on the listening side, where someone acknowledges to you that he or she feels angry—whether or not the anger is aimed at you—you can help by validating their acknowledgment and focusing on their feelings. For example:

- When Erin told Jen and Al that she felt angry about things outside of work, their responses—nodding and saying "Thanks"—showed that they heard what she said about her feelings, understood, and appreciated being told.
- When Erin told Jen she was angry at her, Jen's response—"I understand"—meant she understood how Erin felt. It did not mean she necessarily agreed with what Erin thought happened, but it validated Erin's feelings.
- Jen's second response—"How about getting together at 3 today?"—addressed Erin's request to discuss the issue. The important item here is that Jen made practical arrangements *after* acknowledging Erin's feelings.

- In both situations, in addition to focusing first on Erin's feelings, Jen also reacted in ways that were *not* defensive. Even when the anger was aimed at her, she focused on Erin's feelings and did not try to "explain" or defend herself. Jen's lack of defensiveness allowed the focus to remain on Erin's feelings. Later, during their discussion, any concerns Jen has about her own feelings can be included.

As these examples show, there are two sides to acknowledging anger:

- When others acknowledge someone's anger, the intensity of the anger decreases. Discussion can follow the acknowledgment.
- When someone acknowledges his or her own anger, others can help by responding in ways that are accepting and not defensive. Discussion can follow the acknowledgment and the acceptance of it.

It's also important to notice that even though feelings are being acknowledged:

- they are acknowledged in ways that are supportive but not "emotional" or "personal"
- therefore, the acknowledgment is appropriate for the workplace.

In managing anger, the third skill is to acknowledge the feelings of the angry person—whether it is someone else, or yourself.

6

The Fourth Skill: Something in Common

One reason acknowledgment works, as described in the previous chapter, is that it establishes a bond between the angry person and those who give the acknowledgment. That bond also gives them something in common.

Finding something in common is the fourth skill that helps manage anger. When someone is angry, or two people are in conflict, their *differences* are what stand out the most. They focus on what bothers them about each other, where they disagree, how their goals are different, and other ways in which they oppose, or differ from, each other. When differences are emphasized, the anger increases on both sides and the conflict intensifies. The Behavior Wheel looks like this:

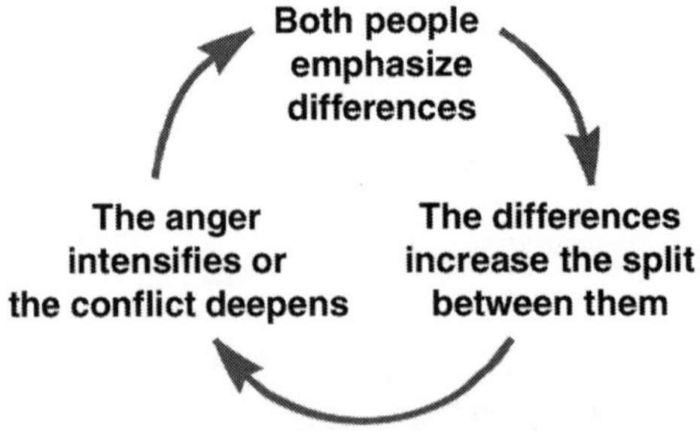

The fourth skill can prevent this from happening.

The Fourth Skill: Finding Something in Common

Even though the differences are real, there also are many things we have in common with the people towards whom we feel angry. At work, you and your co-workers, employees, and managers at least have work in common. You also may share other activities or be friends. When someone feels angry at work, it helps to remember what he or she has in common with the target of the anger. The goal is *not* to deny the anger. The goal is to stay calm enough to get into a discussion with the other person so the issue can be resolved.

Megan was angry. Kathy said something over the phone to a customer that made it sound as if Megan had not done a good job when Megan sold an item to the customer. Who was Kathy to talk, anyway? And why was she complaining to a customer?

Megan felt her face getting hot.

Then she thought about how she and Kathy sometimes listen to each other vent about difficult customers and other frustrations at work. Kathy's job was the same as Megan's. No wonder she understood better than anyone how tough Megan's job could be!

Megan still felt angry towards Kathy, but she also felt calmer than she did a minute ago. She decided that at break, she would talk to Kathy about what bothered her.

Their new Behavior Wheel will look like this:

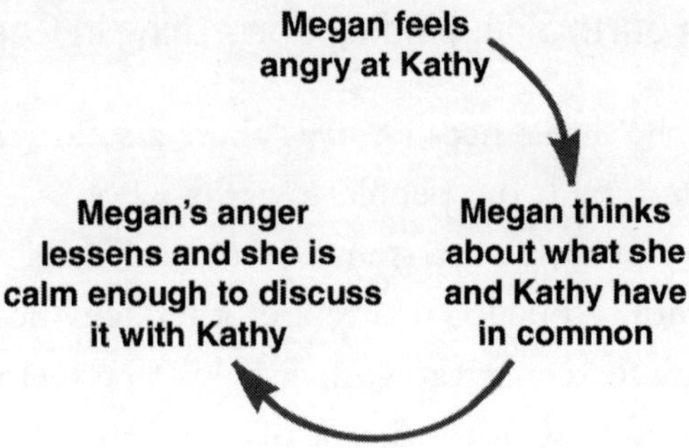

When you are angry at someone, thinking about what you have in common can help prepare you to talk to them about the issue.

If Someone at Work is Angry at You

If you are the target of someone's anger, it helps to remind them that you both have some things in common.

> Raoul was angry at Jasmine. She was late again, and because they were making the presentation together, it made him look bad as well. The customer was nice about it when he called and said there'd be a delay, but there was no excuse for this.
>
> When Jasmine walked in Raoul glared at her. "You're keeping the customer waiting," he said coldly.
>
> "Well, both of us want to look good to the customer," Jasmine replied. "Let's focus on that right now, and talk about the problem afterwards."
>
> Raoul sighed. "All right," he said, "let's do that."

By reminding Raoul that they both had the same goals regarding the customer, Jasmine was able to help him get past his anger *for the moment* and take care of what they needed to do. She also acknowledged the need to talk, and set a general timeframe when they would do it. Their Behavior Wheel looks like this:

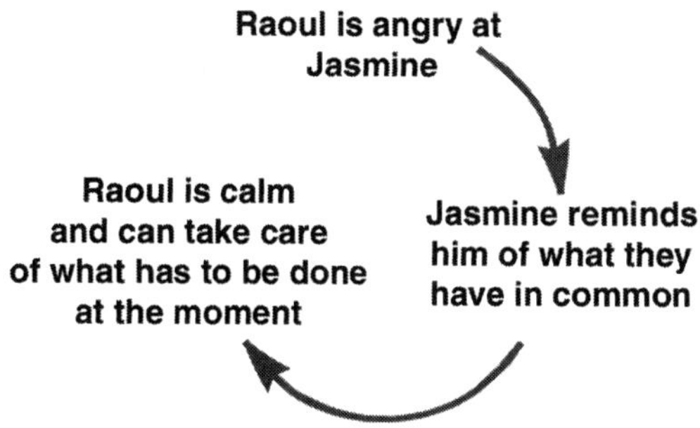

Conflicts

Anger is within an individual, and conflict occurs between two or more people. The skill of finding something in common also is useful in conflict situations.

> Mario found Elwood's low-key, indirect style annoying, because it was never clear to Mario where Elwood stood on any issues.
>
> Elwood found Mario's outspoken, direct style too brash, because he thought Mario was closed to any ideas other than his own. Both men were on the same team, and the meetings were reduced to hostile exchanges between the two of them.
>
> Elwood approached Mario and said, "Our different styles create problems between us. But we both have to remember that our work is judged according to how well our whole team performs."
>
> Mario looked at him and nodded his head in agreement. "Yes," he said. "We have to work towards that goal."

Elwood's comments did not resolve the problem. But the common goal can motivate both men to use a number of the skills in this book, to resolve their conflict. At this point, the common goals establish a "truce." The Behavior Wheel is:

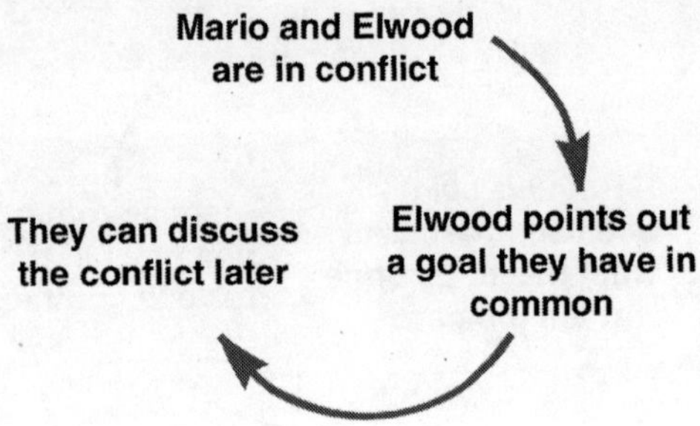

Remember that like acknowledgment, finding something in common does *not* remove the anger or solve the conflict. Both skills allow the degree of hostility to diminish, so the individual or those in conflict will be more willing—later—to discuss, and resolve, the issues.

7

The Fifth Skill: Depersonalizing

A major source of anger and conflict is taking things too personally. Sometimes, comments or events are *intended* to be personal. Other times, we misinterpret neutral comments and hear them in personal ways or we get angry about some assumptions we've made.

Notice the differences between *professional feedback* and *personal attacks:*

- Professional feedback focuses on your work-related behaviors, performance, and results. Personal attacks focus on your motives, personality, personal life, tastes, friends, and other non-work issues.
- The purpose of professional feedback is to improve your work performance, skills, and results. The purpose of personal attacks is to make you feel bad about yourself.

Because these two items are so different, we will react to each of them in very different ways. At work, we have to remember that:

- Assuming it is delivered in a professional and appropriate style, professional feedback can help us learn. We may not agree with it, we may be uncomfortable about not already knowing the new skill, but we understand that the "real issue" behind professional feedback is ever-improving work performance. We rarely feel angry about professional feedback—and when we do, it usually is because we sense some unfairness or inaccuracy.

- Personal attacks are *not* related to work. They are about us as individuals, and they make us question our self-worth, confidence, lovability, and other aspects of our well-being. They threaten us at a primal, subliminal level, and make us feel the negative ways we felt in middle school or high school. Personal attacks easily evoke our anger—and the attackers know this.

The distinction between the two is important, because if we misinterpret professional feedback—or even a neutral, non-issue-related comment—as a personal attack, our anger and other reactions will be inappropriate at work and will make us look unprofessional.

Here are several examples of how easy it is to take things personally:

Matt's boss told him to sign up for a class in conflict-management. It made Matt angry. He wasn't the only one in the department who got into arguments. In fact, it made him even madder that *he* was singled out, when a lot of the time it was the other guys who started it. He felt indignant. If the boss thought he had problems now, he'd *really* give the boss something to complain about.

***

Nancy walked by Jenelle's office where Jenelle and Jacob were talking. As she walked by, Nancy heard Jenelle say, "Nancy can't handle that." Nancy was mad. Jenelle had told Nancy how well she was doing in her new job, and now here Jenelle was, telling Jacob how Nancy couldn't handle something. What a liar Jenelle is! And what was her motive? Why didn't she just come out and tell Nancy about it, without gossiping behind Nancy's back? Nancy was furious.

***

Troy was angry about the performance review Allison, his manager, just gave him. She told him he needed to put more "structure" in his work—finish projects on time, prepare in advance for meetings, and follow through on commitments he'd made. She had no idea what she was dealing with.

Everywhere else he'd worked, Troy had been recognized for his creativity and his ingenious solutions to problems. How could Allison expect him to perform at his best under a rigid set of rules and what she called "structure"? It burned him up just to think about it. She did it as a power move because she was trying to show her boss she could handle her position. Because Troy was new there, he was the easiest one to pick on. He wasn't going to let her use *him* to step on for her career.

***

Megan saw the dirty look Heather gave her as they passed each other in the hall. It really made Megan mad, because Heather knew the right people in the company, and Megan hated the fact that Heather could make her look bad. Even worse, Heather was dating Brad, who broke up with Megan because of Heather. What else did Heather want from her? Megan would be sneaky about it, but she'd find a way to get even with Heather. Heather wasn't going to get away with treating her like that.

In all these examples, the employee takes things very personally and gets angry. The irony, however, is that the "personal affronts" they perceive *may not* be as they appear. For example:

- Matt's boss may have sent *all* the employees to the conflict-management class. Or it may be that everyone is required to take the class and Matt was the only one in his department who had not taken it.
- Jenelle may have told Jacob, "Nancy can't handle that with the small budget she's got right now. We'll have to allocate more money for her."
- Allison may be giving Troy feedback that will build on, and improve the effectiveness of, his creativity.
- Maybe Heather was about to sneeze, or was having trouble with her contact lenses, and the "dirty look" was nothing more than the natural facial contortions that accompany either event.

It may be that in all four situations, the individuals misinterpreted, and read into, what they saw and heard. To the extent that this is the case, they negatively personalized something that was either neutral, positive, or professional. Their anger was very real, but the basis of it was not. It's also possible that their perceptions were accurate. In either case, the skill of *depersonalizing* will help you manage your anger.

Skill Five: Depersonalizing

When we take something personally, we are making several assumptions:

- We really heard what we thought we heard.

- The person is making these comments knowingly and intentionally, to hurt us.
- Other people will believe what this person says about us.
- This person's opinion of us matters.
- The person is saying something about *us*.

Although several or all of these assumptions sometimes may be accurate, most of the time what's really happening is:

- We misinterpret what we hear, or we "fill in" and add to the fragments of conversation we hear.
- The person is making these comments off-handedly, without malice.
- Other people may or may not believe what the other person says, depending on how well they know us, know the other person, and trust the other person's opinion.
- The opinion of this person, as well as the opinions of everyone else we know, "matter" in that we all would like to be well thought-of by everyone. At the same time, this person's opinion usually does *not* matter in terms of consequences—that is, their opinion rarely has any affect on our lives.
- Most important of all, the fact is that when the other person says negative things about us—or about anyone—their comments often reflect more about *them* than about *us*. In the four situations above, ***if*** the four individuals were correct in their perceptions, the following examples show how the negative comments could reflect more on the speakers than on the individuals:

Matt's boss: His emphasis on conflict-management, and his picking on Matt, could indicate that the boss has trouble managing his own conflicts.

Jenelle's lies: Her duplicity shows that she has trouble giving honest feedback to her employees.

Allison's requirements: She is worried that Troy may know more than she does, so she has to find fault with his work. Another possibility is that she needs more structure in her own work style.

Depersonalizing means looking at the situation from a number of possible angles, instead of automatically assuming that your perceptions are accurate. To depersonalize, you must:

- Ask yourself whether what you heard (or think you heard) is related to work, or whether it is a personal attack. If it is related to work, focus on the *work* issues involved and disregard the personal references—this is described in more detail below. If what you heard is *not* related to work, take the next steps described in this list.
- Look at the assumptions you make, look for areas where you may misunderstand, fill-in, or assume too much, and then decide how seriously you should take your belief that you were personally attacked.
- If you still think you *were* personally attacked, think about the possible motives of the attacker. Ask yourself: what's in it for *them,* in attacking you?
- Ask yourself what their attack says about *them,* not about you.

If the Comments Relate to Work

Depersonalizing also means focusing on the work-related issues *without* assessing your personal worthiness, lovability, confidence, and other aspects of your personal life and without feeling bad about yourself. If someone makes what feels like a personal attack, and you think that some of what they said relates to work, sort out those work-related items and treat them as professional feedback. For example:

- Focus on behaviors. What are they telling you about what you do that works really well? What work-related behaviors should you change, to be even more effective?
- Focus on results. What are they telling you about the outcomes you achieve? In what ways could you improve them?
- Focus on work relationships and methods. What are they telling you about how good a team-player you are? How can you be even more helpful?
- Focus on customers. What are they telling you about the impact of your work on customers? What can you do you be more customer-oriented?

You can learn from others' comments by treating them as professional feedback. Everything they say that does not relate to work—that is, everything that feels like a personal attack—you can dismiss as *their* issues, not yours. By depersonalizing in these ways, you are much more likely to learn and much less likely to become angry.

Here are examples of what depersonalizing can look—and feel—like using the situations described above.

Matt's boss told him to sign up for a class in conflict-management. His first reaction was mild annoyance, because of how heavy his workload was. Thinking of this requirement in terms of professional feedback, Matt thought about all the conflicts he'd had or seen at work and realized that having the right skills would make his work a lot easier. His annoyance changed to appreciation that the company offered this kind of training.

***

Nancy walked by Jenelle's office where Jenelle and Jacob were talking. As she walked by, Nancy heard Jenelle say, "Nancy can't handle that." Nancy was upset and wondered what it was she couldn't handle. Interpreting the comment as professional feedback, she mentally reviewed the projects she was working on and all the feedback Jenelle had given her.

"Funny," she thought to herself, "the only thing I'm aware of not being able to handle is my limited budget! I'll have to let Jenelle know I overheard her, and find out what it was she said I can't handle."

***

Troy was angry about the performance review Allison, his manager, just gave him. She told him he needed to put more "structure" in his work—finish projects on time, prepare in advance for meetings, and follow through on commitments he'd made. He saw himself as a very creative, high-producing specialist, and her review conflicted with this image. Treating her input as professional feedback, he thought about the projects he'd worked on since he started this job and realized that when problems had occurred, they were of the type Allison mentioned. His anger subsided as he admitted to himself that he would be more effective if he made these changes.

***

Megan saw the dirty look Heather gave her as they passed each other in the hall. It made Megan angry because she knew Heather resented the fact that Megan was dating her ex-boyfriend. In trying to treat Heather's behavior as professional feedback, Megan realized that this was strictly a personal attack. She decided that it showed how envious, and perhaps even sad, Heather was. Her anger faded as she felt a little sympathy for Heather.

The same principles apply to situations, as well as to comments others make. Here's an example:

Cindy usually had lunch with her supervisor, the manager, and several others from the same department. The lunch group was so casual and friendly that she was surprised to learn that everyone but she had been invited to a party at the manager's house. At first, it hurt her feelings and made her angry. But as she tried to treat the situation as professional feedback, she remembered that the party was the top-management get-together which took place the night before every Board meeting. Cindy realized that invitations depended on one's position, not on how well-liked they were. Her hurt feelings—and her anger—went away.

Anger is natural—and quick to appear—when we feel personally attacked. Depersonalizing helps you tell the difference between real attacks, and professional feedback from which you can learn. The more you can depersonalize, the less anger you'll experience.

When the comments or events are *not* intended as personal, it's even more important for you to avoid taking them that way.

8

The Sixth Skill: Getting to the Real Issues

Mario and Elwood in Chapter 6 established a common goal, but they still could get into conflict if they focus on the wrong issues. For example:

> Mario thought about what Elwood said about them both being judged on how well the team performs. Mario realized that the hostile relationship with Elwood was hurting both of them.
>
> "Remember what you said about how our different styles cause problems between us?" Mario asked Elwood. "Well, I'm really glad you brought that up. You'll need to communicate more like I do, and there won't be so many problems. I'm really glad to help you do it, also."
>
> Elwood was stunned. He was so angry that he couldn't say anything. He was afraid Mario took his silence as agreement.

Mario misses the point and, in the process, alienates Elwood, because his comments imply three things:

- The difference in styles is Elwood's fault.
- Elwood is wrong to communicate the way he does.

- Elwood should change his communication style to what Mario thinks it should be.

Ironically, the original conflict—which is about style differences—has become compounded, and another conflict—about whose "fault" it is, and who has to change—has arisen. So far, their Behavior Wheel looks this way:

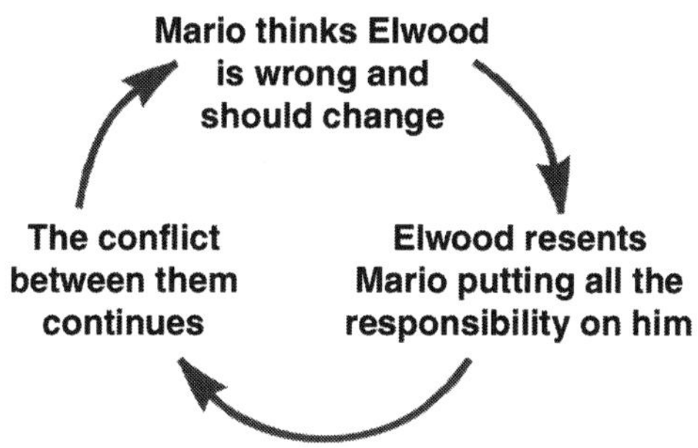

In this situation, the anger will only intensify.

If Mario were to look at the situation more objectively, he would realize that:

- The *differences* in their styles cause problems. One style—in this case, Elwood's—is not, in itself, the problem.
- Both styles are legitimate because there is no such thing as a "right" or "wrong" style. There *are* issues such as timing, circumstances, and misunderstandings.
- To resolve the conflict between them, *both* will have to understand the other's needs, identify when each style works best for the specific circumstances, and discuss other ways each can help the other understand him.

If Mario saw the situation this way, the conversation could have begun like this:

"You know, what you said earlier about our styles being different fits how I see it, too," Mario told Elwood. "What do *you* see as the differences between us?"

"Well," Elwood said, "I see you being more direct and to the point. How to you see me?"

"I see you being more general and open-ended. It's not always clear to me whether you've agreed with something or not."

This time, Mario and Elwood have identified the issue as *differences* in their styles. Their Behavior Wheel looks like this:

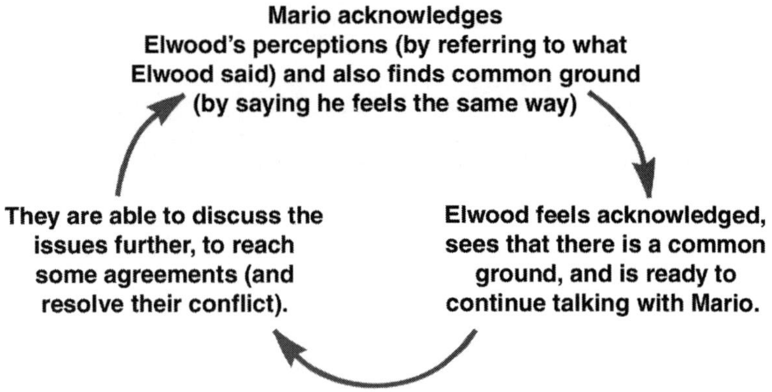

And in this case, Mario and Elwood could discuss the issue and decide what to do to get along better. The anger would subside instead of increasing.

What Makes the Difference

The difference between the first and second example are that in the second example:

- Mario focuses on the real issue (the differences in style) instead of on Elwood's style.

- Mario puts the responsibility on both himself and Elwood, instead of putting it all on Elwood.
- Mario supports and helps Elwood, instead of alienating him.
- Elwood also is able to focus on the real issue, because he does not feel defensive.
- Elwood is able to take his share of the responsibility, because he does not feel alienated.

The key—once feelings are acknowledged and common ground is established—is to get to the real issues.

Skill Six: Getting to the Real Issues

As you probably know from experience, the "real issues" can be hard to identify. Here's an example:

Lisa was mad at Trevor. Sometimes he'd get real enthusiastic when she came up with an idea, but other times he'd totally ignore her. She'd thought at first that his reaction depended on his mood, but he was pretty easygoing most of the time. Now she started thinking that his lack of response meant he thought her ideas were stupid.

Well, if he didn't have the decency to speak up when he didn't like her ideas, why should she go out of her way to get along with him? The company was pushing teamwork, but that meant *all* team members had to take part, not just Lisa. She decided to do the same thing *he* did to her—ignore him back.

Lisa was shocked when, after a few days, Trevor walked over to her desk and asked, "Is something wrong? I notice that you're talking to everyone in the department but me."

"Well," Lisa said, "You ignore me when you don't like my ideas, so I'm just doing the same thing to you."

Trevor looked surprised, and then he smiled.

"Lisa," he said, "I have a hearing problem. Sometimes I don't hear what someone says. Sorry it looked like I was ignoring you."

Lisa saw the Behavior Wheel this way:

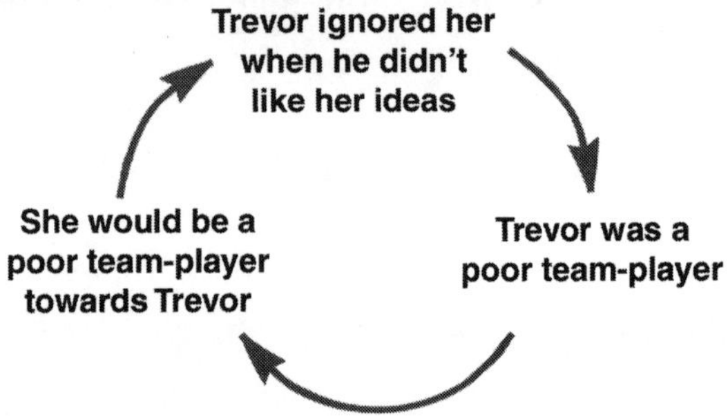

She learned from Trevor that the Behavior Wheel really looked like this:

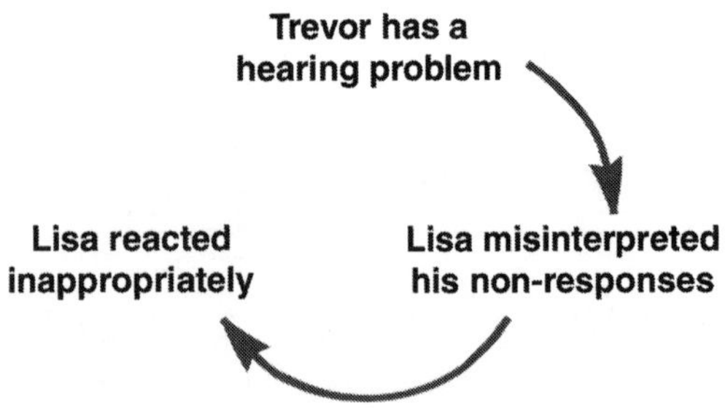

Now, Lisa has the opportunity to make the Behavior Wheel become:

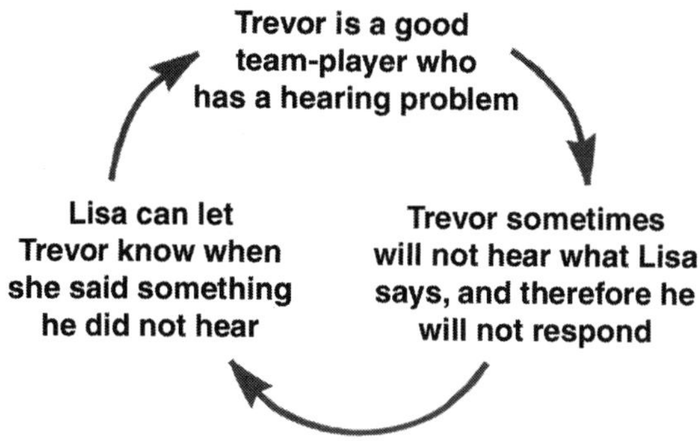

Lisa originally thought the "real issues" were that Trevor:

- at times, intentionally did not respond to her
- ignored her because he did not like her ideas
- therefore was a poor team-player
- deserved to be "ignored back"

In reality, the "real issues" were that Trevor:

- at times did not hear something she said
- was a good team player
- needs her to recognize his silence as an indication that he did not hear her
- needs her to help him make sure he hears what she says.

In what appeared to be a "personal" or "personality" problem, the real issue turned out to be Trevor's hearing problem. And in what appeared to be "poor teamwork," the real issue turned out to be a need for team effort in making sure Trevor hears Lisa (and everyone else).

Insight, but No Obligations

Notice that even if Lisa sees the Behavior Wheel this way, she still has only the *opportunity*—*not* the obligation—to respond as described. Identifying the real issues does not, in itself, resolve anger or conflict. It *does* give everyone the ability to focus on *facts* about each other's reality, instead of on misinterpretations, vague impressions, or assumptions. Once we know what each other really is dealing with, we still have to decide what we want to do. At the same time, when we know the real issues, we are much more likely to respond in ways that eliminate the anger, resolve the conflict, and improve the work relationship.

The work relationship between Lisa and Trevor, their attitudes and feelings, and overall team rapport depends first on how the "real issue" is *defined*—and then, on how each person decides to act.

In this example, it was Trevor who began the process of identifying the real issues because *he* took the initiative and asked Lisa why she ignored him. Lisa could have taken this step herself, by asking *him* the same question.

You May Not Like What the Real Issues Are

Sometimes, the outcome of this kind of discussion may be different from what you hope or want. Even then, at least the outcome will be genuine and authentic because the real issues have been addressed. Here's an example:

> "We've already talked several times about your repeated lateness," Jennifer told Kristen. "I haven't seen any improvement since our last discussion. What's going on?"
>
> "Well, I'm trying," Kristen said.
>
> "What gets in the way?" Jennifer asked.
>
> Kristen was quiet for a moment. Then she said, "You know, Jennifer, I think the problem is that I'm a night person and

have a lot of trouble getting up early. The schedule here doesn't fit what I'm used to or what I like."

By asking what was going on, Jennifer helped Kristen state the real issue. And Jennifer may have been disappointed when she heard what the real issue was, because she'd hoped that Kristen's behavior would change. However, it's important to know the real issue even if we don't like what it is. Jennifer benefits by not having to waste any more time trying to get Kristen to change her behavior.

At the same time, Kristen also gains by stating the real issue, because she no longer has to pretend she'd trying to meet Jennifer's requirements. She may have been keeping this secret all along, or she may have realized what the problem was only after Jennifer asked her. For Kristen, there is relief in recognizing—and stating—that she needs a different job. Whether you are the one asking for the real issue or the one saying what it is, you will be better off.

A Different Perspective

In the examples above, the real issues were the facts, perceptions, interpretations, and feelings regarding certain behaviors. These behaviors had led to anger on the part of those *affected* by them. The behaviors also had created conflict between the person who was affected and the person who carried out the behaviors. In all these cases, the perspective was that of the individuals affected by the behaviors.

We also can look at the real issues from the perspective of the person who *exhibits* behaviors that negatively affect others.

Ray had had it. For more than a year, he'd been working 70 or 75 hours a week. He'd already worked 45 hours in the last three days, and now they were trying to get him to stay longer today. What did they think he was, one of their machines?

Some reward for being responsible and reliable! He'd show them. He threw his tools on the floor, said nothing to anyone, and stormed out of the shop. His machine was still running.

Looking at this situation from Ray's point of view, the real issues are likely to be:

- He's angry at management for pushing him so hard.
- He's physically, and mentally, exhausted from working too many hours.
- He feels "picked on" and pressured by management.
- He's frustrated that being a good worker has led to what he sees as "punishment."
- He feels justified in "getting even."

The fact that these are Ray's real issues—and also the fact that we can identify with them—does not make his behavior acceptable. The point is that these are the issues Ray is expressing through his anger. The Behavior Wheel looks like this:

For a healthier and more productive workplace, the Behavior Wheel would have to change to:

An Angry Co-Worker

You don't have to be a manger to see inappropriate behavior as a signal that the person has real issues to express. In one of the examples above, both Trevor and Lisa had the opportunity to ask about the other's inappropriate behavior. You can do the same when a co-worker's behavior indicates that he or she has issues with you.

One limitation, however, is the degree of anger your co-worker expresses. The closer an individual comes to violence, the greater the need for you to go to your manager, Human Resources, the Employee Assistance Program, or other counseling services, security, and even the police.

An Angry Manager

You may know managers above you who express their anger in inappropriate ways. Because they have more authority than you, you are not in a position to get into discussions with them about their real issues. Instead, it would be more effective to talk to another manager about your concerns. The manager you confide in can take the appropriate actions.

Another Part of Getting to the Real Issues

Getting to the real issues includes one more item: *how* a person says what he or she says. This is true whether the speaker is the angry person trying to express his or her real issues, or someone else who is asking the angry person what the real issues are.

Here's an example of trying to express the real issues behind one's anger:

Tim was furious. His manager had interrupted him again while he as helping a customer, and it made Tim look like he didn't know how to do his job. Tim decided it was time to have one of those "talks" the manager kept saying they should have when Tim had a problem.

"Thanks a lot for your show of confidence in me," Tim said sarcastically. "You really know how to motivate employees, don't you?"

His manager looked at him. "Leave this office," the manager said, "and come back when you're calm enough to talk."

Tim's real issues were:

- He felt foolish when his manager spoke to him in front of customers.
- The manager has done this before.
- He's angry at the manager for making him look bad.

But his *way* of talking makes it impossible for him to discuss these issues with his manager. The manager very likely sees Tim's comments as another inappropriate expression of Tim's anger. Tim is working against himself, as this Behavior Wheel shows:

To be able to discuss his real issues with is manager, Tim would have to talk in the following ways:

- Use a pleasant tone, to create an environment that is cooperative.
- Talk in a straightforward manner that shows respect.
- Avoid accusations about the manager's intentions.
- Start by stating his goal or purpose, and focus on his own feelings and needs instead of on what the manager did wrong. For example, "I want to talk with you about a problem I have," or "I'd like to talk to you about some help I need from you."
- Describe, in factual ways, the specific things that bothered him. For example, "I felt like I looked foolish when you interrupted me while I was with a customer."
- Be prepared to suggest solutions. For example, if the manager asks Tim what he wanted for the future, Tim could say, "I'd like you to either leave me a message to come see you or, out on the floor, wait until I'm done with the customer."

This approach would have allowed Tim to discuss his real issues with his manager. This approach requires the angry person to:

- wait until he or she is calm enough to talk reasonably.
- know specifically what he or she is angry about.
- know what he or she wants changed.

Here's an example of trying to find out the real issues, from someone who is angry:

> Rachel knew Tim was angry. She knew it had something to do with his manager, and she'd hoped he would come talk to her about it. But several hours had gone by already. She decided to go ask him what was wrong.
>
> "Do you want to talk? It looks like you're getting on your boss's nerves again."
>
> Tim's face got red and Rachel could see how angry he was. He swore at her and told her to leave.

Even though Rachel meant well, the way she spoke to Tim only angered him further. This Behavior Wheel shows what happened:

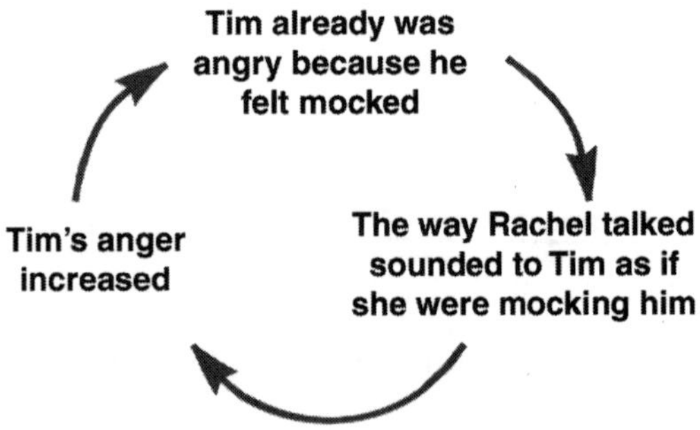

To be able to help Tim, Rachel would have to:

- Acknowledge his feelings. For example, she can say, "You look upset" or "You look angry."

- State her goal of wanting to help him. For example, she could start by saying, "You seem angry and I'd like to help you. I can listen, if you'd like to talk."
- Show respect for what he wants to do. If he says he is not ready to talk, she can say, "Okay. I'm glad to listen whenever you're ready" and leave him alone. If he is ready to talk, she should listen without giving opinions. She also can acknowledge the feelings he expresses, simply by nodding her head or saying, for example, "It sounds like you felt foolish in the customer's eyes."

This approach would have allowed Tim to talk with Rachel about the real issues—if he wanted to.

Getting to the real issues helps you get past misinterpretations, vague impressions, and assumptions and enables you to deal with facts about everyone's reality. With this information, you can choose the best ways to respond.

9

The Seventh Skill: Letting Go

The six anger-management skills you've seen so far empower you to do everything *you* can do. You've decided that you, and they,want to work things out—at least to some degree. You have gone directly to the appropriate person, acknowledged anger and other feelings (yours, theirs, or both), found something in common between the two of you, depersonalized the situation, and identified the real issues. Now, you have to use the hardest skill—letting go.

Letting go means drawing a line between what you can, will, want to, think you should, or are willing to do, and what is *out of your hands* and up to the other person. This sounds easier than it is, because it can be a situation where we *know* something is out of our control but we *want* to try to control it anyway. The contrast between what we know and what we feel can be frustrating. It can make us do things even when we know better.

In anger and conflict, the need to let go means that even though you've taken all these steps, you still can't *make* the other person do what you want and you can't *make* things turn out the way you want. What you've done is *allow* for what you want to happen—and the response is in the other person's hands.

Marla and Carrie had stopped talking to each other more than a year ago. Marla no longer remembered the original reason, but she often thought about how the distance between them kept getting wider and wider. They used to have lunch together and occasionally go places on the weekends, but now they did not even say hello when they passed each other in the hallway.

Marla decided to try to re-establish the friendship. She left Carrie a note that said:

"Carrie, I'd like to apologize for my part of our long silence. I'd like us to start talking to each other again. It's felt strange to not even say hello, and maybe you've felt the same way. I don't even remember the reasons we stopped, but we can talk them over if you'd like to. Please let me know if you'd like to meet for coffee or lunch. I'm at the same number, #6358."

Marla knew Carrie got the note, because it was in with the rest of Carrie's mail. But she never heard back from Carrie, and when they passed in the hall, Carrie still looked the other way.

Marla stated her goals and purposes, acknowledged her own feelings and referred to Carrie's feelings, and got to the real issues. For whatever reason, Carrie did not respond. Marla did all that she could, but she can't reconnect with Carrie because Carrie does not want to. Marla now has to let go.

Letting go has several parts to it:

- feelings of helplessness, because there is nothing else you can do
- feelings of sadness, because of lost opportunities

- feelings of fear, because for this moment we are so painfully aware of how little control we have over our lives
- feelings of guilt, because the other person's refusal to cooperate may be due to something we did
- and of course, feelings of anger, because we did not get what we wanted.

Everyone experiences these feelings in different ways. Healthy ways—described in the last part of this chapter—allow us to stay in touch with our feelings and go on. But people who exhibit the eight inappropriate forms of anger refuse to let go, which means they lose touch with what they really feel and carry old hurts and grudges that become more intense over time.

Here are examples of the ways in which these employees and managers avoid letting go.

Acted-Out Anger

To employees, co-workers, and managers who exhibit Acted-Out Anger, letting go means failing—and it evokes their rage.

> When it was clear that Heather, from sales, wouldn't go out with him, Matt was furious. He couldn't take "no." He ran out to the parking lot, searched hurriedly for her car, and in front of everyone in the lot, broke her window and slashed all four tires. That'll keep her from going *anywhere,* he thought to himself.

Matt acted out his anger instead of going through the pain of letting go. He ignored his feelings of loss by hiding behind his anger.

Unconnected Anger

Instead of letting go, these individuals blame others when they don't get what they want.

> Saveena was overlooked for a new position in her department because she was late almost every day. She'd applied for the job, but when her co-worker got it, she shrugged her shoulders. Oh well, she thought, I guess it all depends on who you know.

Saveena replaced the letting-go process with blame. As a person who takes no responsibility for her actions, she could not even take ownership of her losses and disappointments.

Self-Centered Anger

Employees and managers who exhibit Self-Centered Anger ignore the need to let go by finding other things to want for themselves.

> Andy took over the meetings whether he knew anything about the issues or not. His co-workers were glad when he was taken off the team and put on a "special project." They weren't surprised when they found out that Andy had alienated everyone else working on the project.
>
> Among other things, their complaint was that he insisted on moving the meetings to his area, even though everyone else worked in the other building.

On the surface, it may look like Andy simply moved from one team to the other. The truth is that he ignored his feelings of loss when he was removed from the first team, by using the new project as a distraction—and as another place to make demands on people.

Undercover Anger

Just as they express their anger covertly, these employees and managers also avoid acknowledging their losses by using covert actions.

> Linda didn't like hearing that she wouldn't be going to the conference. It was even worse when she found out that Kathy was going. The boss favored Kathy in a lot of ways, and Linda knew that the conference would give Kathy even more opportunities for advancement. On the morning Kathy left for Houston, Linda called the hotel and canceled Kathy's reservation.

Instead of acknowledging her own pain and disappointment, Linda took her pain out on Kathy—secretly.

Rigid Anger

Those who exhibit Rigid Anger tend to control people and circumstances as their way of avoiding letting go.

> The company lost the bid on a big project everyone had been counting on. Jamal, who had put the bid together, knew exactly what went wrong—he had listened to the input of several others on the team, instead of insisting on what he knew was right. Well, *that* would never happen again! From now on, he would tell the team what to do regarding the bids, and they would have to go along with whatever he said. Jamal almost appeared gleeful as he told the team that the company would have gotten the bid if the team had only listened to him.

For Jamal, being in control and being "right" enables him to avoid the pain of not always winning.

Escapist Anger

For these individuals, avoiding reality in general enables them to avoid letting go.

> Jeff liked to feel confident and capable, and it only took a few hits to make him feel that way. The day he lost his job, because of absenteeism and falling asleep on the job, he took even more hits than usual. After a while, he started to think about what to tell his wife about why he wasn't going to work anymore.

Jeff shut his feelings off very literally—and chemically. He avoids letting go emotionally by "letting go" of reality for the moment.

Shocking Anger

When these employees and managers want to avoid letting go, they do it by going to extremes.

> Susan had hoped her temp job would become permanent. She'd been her most professional every day. But she found out today that she'd be leaving at the end of the week. It was too bad, because this was the best assignment she'd had.
>
> Well, it didn't matter anymore, so she could be her real self. No more "professional" stuff. The next day, she brought her radio and wore jeans. What were they going to do, fire her?

Susan's out-of-character behavior is her way of avoiding her need to let go. She hides her pain behind her unexpected behavior.

Strange Anger

Individuals who exhibit Strange Anger are less able than most of us to deal with loss and letting go. They tend to experience the pain of loss as something coming from outside, instead of as feelings coming from within.

> Dina's favorite manager was leaving. She noticed that ever since he announced his retirement, her co-workers started putting more pressure on her. They were more critical, they talked about her behind her back, and they made fun of her. Worse, they did it so subtly that no one else knew except her. They appeared to be doing and saying normal things, but their tones of voice and their facial expressions gave them away.

Dina experiences her emotional pain as if it were being imposed on her, and she is hypersensitive to her co-workers. Without any awareness on her part, Dina's delusions are blocking her pain and her need to let go.

Healthy Letting Go

In all eight examples, the employees and managers block their pain, and their need to let go—and it works for them, in the short-term. But in the long-term, they lose touch with themselves and they never heal from their losses or disappointments. Even worse, they carry grudges and hurts for life. Ironically, their anger intensifies and becomes less manageable as their grudges and pain increase.

There are healthy ways to deal with pain, and truly let go.

- Take steps to do what you can—such as using the anger-management skills.

- Admit, to yourself, that you feel hurt, disappointed, sad—or whatever you feel when things don't go your way.
- Let yourself feel the pain, without doing anything about it. This helps you let go of the urge—or the need—to control it.
- Give others the space to make their own choices. This helps you let go of the urge to control *them.*
- Get on with what you have, and learn to do without what you don't have.

Letting go will make it easier to manager your own, and others', anger.

10

When *They're* Angry at *You*

You've seen seven skills that can help you express *your* anger in reasonable ways:

- Deciding whether the other person really wants to work things out with you
- Acknowledging feelings
- Finding something in common
- Identifying the real issues
- Depersonalizing
- Being direct
- Letting go

When someone is angry at *you*, these skills can help you lower the intensity of their anger. Remember that your goal is not to get rid of anger—it's to help the other person express his or her anger more calmly, so the two of you can solve the problem. With each of the eight inappropriate types of anger, you'll use the same skills in different ways.

Acted-Out Anger

Julian is furious at you. He swears at you and yells, "That's the stupidest thing I've ever seen. How could you do something like that?" He slams his fist against his desk, the veins in his temples pulsating. "*Answer me!* How could you do something so *stupid?*"

Your reactions can reduce his hostility. You can use the seven skills to identify several options regarding your reactions.

Decide whether Julian wants to work things out with you

- He probably does—or will, later. Right now he is venting, at your emotional expense.

Being Direct

- You can speak to Julian right now.
- You can leave and wait until he calms down, and then speak to him.
- Talk to him before saying anything to anyone else. (And maybe you shouldn't say anything to others even afterwards.)

Acknowledge *his* Feelings

- "I can see that you're angry."
- "It's clear that you think what I did was stupid."

Bland as these choices sound, either will lower his intensity a little. Even if he answers "I sure am" or "I sure do," it is likely to be with less hostility than he's showing right now.

Finding Something in Common

- "I agree that I could have done a better job."
- "I agree that there were other ways I could have done it."

You haven't given in, and you haven't said that you go along with everything he's said. You're simply agreeing that this is not the best you've ever done or not the only method you could have used. His intensity most likely will diminish a little more.

Depersonalize

- "What I *did* may have seemed stupid at the time. But *I'm* not stupid."

You're helping Julian separate you, the whole person, from the specific thing you did. This separation will decrease the intensity of his anger even more.

At the same time, you don't have to take his comments personally. He is venting, your specific action is the real target, and you don't have to buy into his sweeping accusations.

Identifying the Real Issues

- "I'd like to discuss this with you, but I can't do it while you're yelling and pounding on the desk."

You have just addressed your first real issue: the way he's talking to you. By staying calm and objectively describing what he's doing—instead of getting angry back at him—you are clearly more in control of yourself than he is of himself. His hostility will again decrease.

If he calms down a lot and reasonably says something like "You're right. Sure, let's talk about it," you can go your next real issue:

- "I would have done it another way, but the deadline didn't allow it. What I did was the best choice for the short time we had left."

If he does *not* calm down enough or sound reasonable enough, stop at your first real issue. Come back to this one later, or another time, when he is ready to talk.

Letting Go

- Your goal is to help Julian calm down enough to speak—and listen—to you reasonably.
- Once he calms down enough, and you've expressed your real issues, you've given him a chance to discuss what bothers him.
- There is no guarantee that Julian will discuss the issues with you or, if he does, that it will turn out the way you want.
- You will have done all you can to lower his level of hostility in this situation.

Unconnected Anger

You've just finished reporting to your co-workers and manager about the status of the project your team is working on. There had been some delays, partly because of slow responses from vendors and partly because of clashes between two of the team members, but you didn't get into any details. You simply said the project would be done two weeks later than scheduled.

Suddenly, Geneen, one of the teammates involved in the conflicts, burst out with, "It's *your* fault that we're not finished yet! *You're* the one who's holding us up, with all the delays."

She folded her arms in front of her and leaned back in her chair.

Decide Whether Geneen Wants to Work Things Out with You

- She may not. She may be trying to one-up you.
- You must give her some kind of response, to maintain your credibility with all your co-workers and your manager.
- Although this may be a stretch, Geneen *could* look interested in getting the project done, so you have to respond in case this is how she comes across.

Be Direct

- She's verbally attacked you in public, and you must respond immediately.
- Your credibility will soar if you respond in a calm and reasonable manner.
- You could simply say, "Let's talk privately." However, because she made it public, you may be better off responding publicly.

Acknowledge *her* Feelings

- "It sounds like you're angry about the delay, and at me for causing it." Her hostility is likely to decrease somewhat. Notice that you're reflecting what she said—you are neither agreeing or disagreeing about whether you caused the delay. That will come up under the real issues.

Finding Something in Common

- "Both of us—and, in fact, the whole team—would like to hve finished sooner. We're all still working hard at it."

You're reminding Geneen—and assuring everyone else—that the whole team is involved, it's not just the two of you, and that finishing quickly is a shared goal. Geneen's anger is likely to become less intense.

Depersonalize

- "I understand your frustration about the delay. But I'm surprised to hear that you blame me for it."

You are helping Geneen—and everyone else—separate the delay from you as a person and as a team leader.

Identify the Real Issues

- "There were two reasons for the delay. One was that several vendors took longer than they'd promised to get materials to us. The other is that there were some communication problems among several team members. I think both those problems have been resolved, but we're dealing now with the impact of them."

Letting Go

- You're being factual, reasonable, and optimistic.
- Geneen's anger has to subside, or she will look foolish.

- As an added irony, your reference to "communication problems among several team members" allows those who know to appreciate how inappropriate Geneen's comments were.
- Even to those who don't know she was involved in the problem, your description explains the problem and shows you are not responsible for the delay.
- You still cannot control what your co-workers or managers (or Geneen) will think.
- You've done everything you can to lower the intensity of her anger.

Self-Centered Anger

Jenny was on call, so she shouldn't have been so annoyed when you paged her. It's part of her job. You told her three machines broke down tonight and you needed her to come fix them.

"You've got a lot of nerve calling me at this hour of the night!" she yelled into the phone. "I've had the flu and needed some rest, and now you woke me up! Why don't you just leave me alone?"

Decide Whether Jenny Wants to Work Things Out with You

- What she wants to work out is that you'll leave her alone.
- You have to try to work it out with her anyway. If you simply say, "Because you're on night shift, and you're on call, and this is your job," she'll only get angrier—and you'll still have machines that aren't working.

Be Direct

- Jenny is the one to talk to.
- If you're her co-worker, and not her manager, you later may want to tell her manager about her reaction. But right now you have to deal directly with Jenny.

Acknowledge *her* Feelings

- "It sounds like you feel pretty bad."

She's not likely to stay as angry when you acknowledge what she feels.

Find Something in Common

- "I'd want to stay home too if I just got over the flu. But we both know that the machines have to get fixed, too."

Jenny will still be annoyed, but her level of hostility will keep declining.

Depersonalize

- "I'm not picking on you, Jenny. It's just that you're the one on call tonight."

You're showing Jenny that you're calling her for work-related, not personal, reasons. Her anger will get even less intense as she realizes that what you say is accurate.

Identify the Real Issues

- "If you're too sick to be on call, your name shouldn't be on the list tonight. Was this a mistake?"

You're showing some sympathy, and also giving Jenny a chance to either say it was a mistake or acknowledge that she is, in fact, well enough to be working. Her anger should have subsided by now.

Letting Go

- Her anger has diminished, so she is less likely to take the request personally.
- Jenny still may not show up.
- If she doesn't arrive, you or her manager can treat her behavior as a performance issue.
- You've done everything you can to get her there and to reduce her anger.

Undercover Anger

> By the time you found out, it was too late. Todd said he'd leave your messages on your desk, as he always did when you were at a client's. It wasn't until you came in this morning and saw the empty desktop that you realized there was a problem. Of course—Todd was angry because you said you couldn't carpool with him.

Decide Whether Todd Wants to Work Things Out with You

- Right now he doesn't.
- He will have to, because your jobs are inter-dependent.

Be Direct

- You have to stand up for yourself, so you must talk to him.
- Because he is not angry *at the moment,* you have to let him know that you have reason to think he *was* angry at you earlier.
- If this is the first time, you should discuss it with Todd and not tell anyone else about it.
- If this is a pattern, you may want to talk to your manager and Todd's because Todd's way of "getting even" interferes with work.

Acknowledge *his* Feelings

- "I saw that you didn't leave me my messages. It must mean that you felt angry."

You are telling him what happened and what you took it to mean about his feelings. In case there was a legitimate reason, Todd has the opportunity to say, "Oh, no, there weren't any. I'm not angry." But he also has the opportunity to tell you *now* that he was angry—and why. Whether he uses this opportunity or not, his anger is likely to decrease because you are giving him a chance to express it.

- "I know you're angry that I can't carpool with you."

When you know this is the cause of his anger—and maybe if you just suspect it—you can acknowledge his feelings.

Find Something in Common

- "We both want to get to work the easiest and least expensive way."

This comment looks for common ground regarding carpooling—the issue about which Todd is angry.

- "We both also would benefit from telling each other when and why we're angry."

This comment allows you to address the issue of Todd's secretive way of expressing his anger.

Depersonalize

- "My inability to carpool with you is not personal. It has to do with my schedule."
- "At the same time, *you* don't have to get personal when you're angry."

With both comments, you're trying to help Todd see the difference between work issues and his anger.

Identify the Real Issues

- "I respect your right to feel angry. But I have a problem with the secretive way you express it."
- "I'd also like to tell you more about why I can't carpool with you. It's because I'll be having some appointments after work for a while that will interfere with your schedule."

Todd's anger should have subsided by now. You have the chance to help him see that issues can be resolved only if everyone knows what they are. Only when he understands this can you get to the carpooling issue.

Letting Go

- You may be able to resolve the carpool issue.
- You may be able to get Todd to understand that he—as well as you—will benefit from him being open about being angry.
- You cannot control how he will act the next time he's angry.
- You've done everything you can to make him aware of better ways to express his anger—and to resolve the current issue.

Rigid Anger

Will marched over to you and you could tell he was mad. You figured it was about the way you solved the scheduling problem. He'd told you to solve it, but you knew he really meant to solve it the way *he* would. So the fact that you did it in a way that made everyone happy about their schedule probably didn't matter to him. Neither did the fact that the whole department already was looking more productive. As Will got closer, you could tell that he was *really* angry.

"What did you do to the schedule?" he yelled. "You know how I like it to work! I needed you to fix a few glitches, but that didn't mean you had to change the whole thing! I've always done it the way I do it and there's no need to change the whole process. My way works!"

Decide whether Will wants to work things out with you

- It doesn't sound like it.
- He *does* want you to do things his way.

- Because you report to him, *you* have to try to work things out with *him*.

Be Direct

- He's the one to talk to.
- It will help your credibility to explain why you did what you did—but this does *not* mean you have to justify your actions.

Acknowledge *his* Feelings

- "I can see that you're angry about the way I did the schedule."

Remember that even though he is likely to answer "You bet I am. I just said so!", acknowledging his feelings will lower his hostility somewhat. Your purpose is to start the process of lowering the intensity of his anger.

Your goal is to help Will become reasonable enough to talk—and listen—to you.

Find Something in Common

- "We both want the schedule to work for everyone."

This is true. However, notice that you intentionally are leaving out the fact that Will wants *his* schedule to work for everyone. Your goal is to find where you both agree, and the one thing you are able to find in common is that you both want a schedule that works.

Depersonalize

- "I wasn't criticizing your schedule when I did things differently."

You want Will to see the scheduling as a *practical* , not personal, issue. He's taking things personally, and his anger will be less intense if he recognizes the difference.

Identifying the Real Issues

- "The problems required some flexibility. The usual scheduling rotations were not going to work."
- "I had to find ways to cover nights differently, because the usual people had to be gone."
- "You asked me to solve the problems, and what I did worked. That's why I don't understand why you're angry."

By now, Will's anger should have diminished. Your clear, objective description of what happened puts Will in a position where he really has only two choices: acknowledge that you did a good job with the schedule, or admit that having it *his* way matters more than how effective it was.

Letting Go

- Just because it *should* turn out this way does not mean it *will.*
- Regardless of Will's reaction, you (and your co-workers) know what really happened.
- You've done everything you can to reduce Will's anger.

Escapist Anger

Nobody knew for sure if Dave used drugs or alcohol, but everyone suspected it because of his moods, frequent absences, and fluctuations in the quality of his work. Now he was angry at you because you didn't cover for him when he came in late again. Where he got the idea that you should cover for him was a mystery to you—you'd never done it before, and you never said you would. But there he stood, telling you how mad he was.

"I got in trouble because you didn't back up what I told the boss!" Dave yelled. "What are you trying to do to me? All you had to do was say 'yes' when they asked you if I was here on time that morning. What's your problem? Why did you get me in trouble?"

Decide Whether Dave Wants to Work Things Out with You

- He doesn't.
- He wants you to give in to his demands.
- You have to stand up for yourself.

Be Direct

- It is important to respond to Dave.
- Under certain conditions—such as if Dave appears to be under the influence of something at the moment, or if you feel unsafe in general with him—it may be more important to remove yourself and go to someone with authority, wait until others are around, or tell Dave you'll talk to him when he is calmer—and then remove yourself.

- In this example, we'll assume that Dave is calm enough, and/or enough other people are around, for you to respond.

Acknowledge *his* Feelings

- "I can see that you're angry because I didn't cover for you."

Remember that your goal is to lower the intensity of his anger.

Finding Something in Common

- "We both work together."
- "We both want to look good to the boss."

Notice that you are *not* pretending Dave wants to do a good job or work as a team member. Instead, you are finding something in yourself that matches his real goals—looking good to the boss—that relates to what he's angry about.

Depersonalize

- "I wasn't trying to do anything to *you.* I was being honest to the boss, which is how I am."
- "My purpose was to tell the truth, which I always try to do. It wasn't to get you in trouble."

You are emphasizing what your intentions were and were not. You also are introducing to Dave a concept that may be new to him: that someone else (you) can have goals that do not relate to him. Your purpose is to help Dave separate what you did (for yourself) from what he suspects your motives were (to "get" him).

The more quickly Dave makes this separation, the faster his anger will subside.

Identify the Real Issues

- "The problem is that I have to tell the truth to the boss, because of my own values, and I can't control what that truth is."
- "It's not my fault that the truth was you weren't here on time."
- "And another issue I'm curious about is why you thought I *would* cover for you instead of telling the truth. Did I ever say I would, or have I done it before?"

You're being straightforward about the reality of it. Dave has the option of clarifying ("Well, I just assumed you would"), staying angry, or accepting that you will not cover for him.

Letting Go

- You cannot control which way Dave goes.
- You may have to go to the manager, Human Resources, the Employee Assistance Program, or others to notify them about Dave's behavior towards you. The purpose would be to make everyone aware in case Dave's anger escalates.
- You've done everything you can to lower the intensity of his anger in this situation.

Shocking Anger

If it were anyone else, you would understand. But to have Kim getting angry at you like this was, well, amazing. She always worked quietly, was pretty mousy, never said anything at meetings, and here she was in your face.

"I will *not* work at night!" she shouted at you. "They told me you and I were switching shifts, and I *will not* do that! If you'd just stay on your shift, there wouldn't be any problems! You have to stay on night shift!" You had never seen her come across so forcefully, and you're stunned.

Decide Whether Kim Wants to Work Things Out with You

- Not really.
- She's trying to tell you what to do—for *her* sake.

Be Direct

- You have the option of refusing to answer her. This may work in the short-run, but in the long run you will have to deal with her.
- Because she is a co-worker and it's always better to get along with everyone, it's worth talking to her.

Acknowledge *her* Feelings

- "I see that you are upset about moving to night shift."
- "And you see it as my fault."

You are taking steps to lower the intensity of her anger.

Finding Something in Common

- "We both work here."

Depersonalize

- "I'm not doing this *to* you."

- "And I'm also not the one who picks my replacement."

You are not justifying anything. You're trying to help Kim separate the appropriate steps you are taking for yourself from her assignment to night shift. She is blurring the two events and holding you responsible.

Identify the Real Issues

- "The company has a policy about night shift, and now it's time for me to go back to days. It has nothing to do with you."
- "The manager chooses my replacement. I don't. I'm not responsible for the manager picking you."
- "If you have a problem with night shift, the manager is the person to see."
- "You can't expect me to base my career plans on *you*."

You're being clear and to the point. Now Kim has to decide what to do.

Letting Go

- You can't control how Kim feels.
- You don't have to listen—or explain—to her again, regarding the night shift.
- You've stood up for yourself.
- You've done everything you can to lower her hostility.

Strange Anger

Josie was in another one of her moods today. She had spent most of the morning in Alex's office, sobbing, complaining, and saying her co-workers were against her because they were all jealous of her. She did this three or four times a week. Why Alex put up with it was beyond you—but you were tired of having to make up for all the work she didn't get done.

You felt very justified when you said to her, "I've had to take care of three of your reports this week, in addition to my own. I can't keep doing this."

And even though you knew you should have been used to it by now, you were still caught off guard by her response.

"I am *so* tired of everyone picking on me!" she said.

"I'm the only one here who is really professional." She started crying. "The rest of you just whine and complain about me all the time! It's all your fault that I get upset!"

Decide Whether Josie Wants to Work Things Out with You

- She clearly does not
- You have to do something with her

Be Direct

- Regarding your work problem, you'll have to see your manager. Josie is *not* the person to talk to about work issues.
- Regarding your relationship with her as a co-worker, you have to do something about the way she treats you.

Acknowledge *her* Feelings

- "I know you feel very emotional."
- "And I know I'm one of the people you blame for it."

You are intentionally focusing on Josie's emotionalism and *not* on *what* she said. Like everyone who exhibits Strange Anger, Josie is overwhelmed by feelings that do *not* necessarily relate to what's really happening around her. She also overreacts to situations that *are* real. So you are not going to get a reasonable discussion of the work issue—or even of whether or not everyone is picking on her.

The best you can do is focus on her feelings and on the fact that she blames you for them.

Find Something in Common

- "We both want you to be happy."
- "We both know that I'm only human."

You are purposely picking common ground that centers on Josie and also reminds her that you, too, are human. On the one hand, you are focusing on what matters most to her—her feelings—and at the same time, you are helping her remember that you, too, have your own feelings.

Depersonalize

- "I know you don't mean that you think I have the power to make you feel bad."
- "Sometimes my own needs may get in the way of what you want. But it doesn't mean I'm doing it *to* you."

In the first comment, you are helping shape the way Josie sees you. Notice that this is the only case in which you "dictate" what the other person "should" think or feel, by talking as if you assume they already think or feel this way. The reason is that Josie's emotionalism is very unstable and you must guide her towards learning what she needs to know.

In the second comment, you are asserting the fact that you, too, have needs and feelings and that they are separate from her.

Identify the Real Issues

- You feel bad sometimes, and you want to blame it on me. But you have to ask yourself what *your* part of it is, also.
- I acknowledge that sometimes I do things you don't like. But you also have to acknowledge that *you* sometimes do things *I* don't like.
- It would be great if you and I could talk about *both* my part of it *and* yours.

You have explained things accurately. Josie's anger probably has subsided by now, although she also may have started crying at this point.

She has to decide how to react to what you said.

Letting Go

- Individuals who exhibit Strange Anger usually are not capable of sustaining reasonable moods or seeing things from anyone's point of view but their own.
- Josie is not likely to keep up her part of the discussions you describe, although she may try to for a while.

- She will become less angry, and more reasonable, each time you respond to her outbursts this way. But you cannot expect these improvements to last very long.
- You will have to see your manager about Josie's failure to do her work and the impact on your workload. Your manager will have to monitor Josie's behavior, as well as task-performance, because of Josie's overwhelming emotionalism.
- You've done everything you can to lower Josie's anger in this situation.

When co-workers, employees, or managers express their anger in the eight inappropriate ways, you can take steps to lower their intensity at that moment.

11

Preventing Acted-Out Anger

We've seen seven skills for managing anger and conflict. These include:

- Deciding whether the other person really wants to work things out with us
- Acknowledging feelings
- Finding something in common
- Identifying the real issues
- Depersonalizing
- Being direct
- Letting go

So far, we've focused on the seven skills in terms of each of us managing our own anger. At the same time, it's important to remember that *our reactions* to the anger of our co-workers, employees, and managers can influence the ways *they* manage it. When we see the eight types of inappropriate anger at work, we can help by using the seven skills.

Interestingly, however, employees and managers who express anger in the eight inappropriate ways also tend to display specific problem behaviors even when they're *not* angry. Under "normal" (non-angry) circumstances, certain problem behaviors are unique to each of the eight inappropriate ways of expressing anger. Knowing this allows you to see, in advance, these individuals' tendencies towards inappropriate types of anger, so you can use the seven skills with them *even when they're not angry.* By using the skills in advance, you are likely to help prevent them from expressing their anger inappropriately and help guide them toward expressing it in ways that work.

To effectively use these skills in advance, you have to consider which type of anger the individual tends to demonstrate and which category of disruptive behaviors he or she typically exhibits. Each of the eight types of inappropriate anger (and the related disruptive behaviors) requires a different emphasis when you use the seven skills.

In this and the next several chapters, we're going to see how to use the seven skills to counter the eight inappropriate types of anger *before* they occur. Later, we'll see how to use these skills when the individuals *exhibit* their anger in the eight inappropriate ways.

Countering Acted-Out Anger Before It Occurs

In Acted-Out Anger, the co-workers, employees, or managers make it clear they are angry, but do nothing to solve the problem. When they are angry, their behaviors can range from yelling, screaming, slamming doors, pounding desks, and throwing things to stomping out of meetings, pouting, or refusing to participate in discussions. Whether they overreact or withdraw, they make it clear that they are angry.

But even when they're *not* angry, those who display Acted-Out Anger tend to disrupt work in specific ways. They tend to:

- be impulsive
- have exaggerated mood swings
- overreact when problems occur.

For example:

Neal could be creative, but he also could be pretty disruptive. During one meeting, he got what he called "this great idea" and led the whole team off on a tangent for the rest of the meeting.

Another time, he came up with a customer-service plan that was completely unworkable. At times, when he was in one of his "terrific" moods, he'd ask customers personal questions that popped into his head as he talked to them.

The Behavior Wheel looks like this:

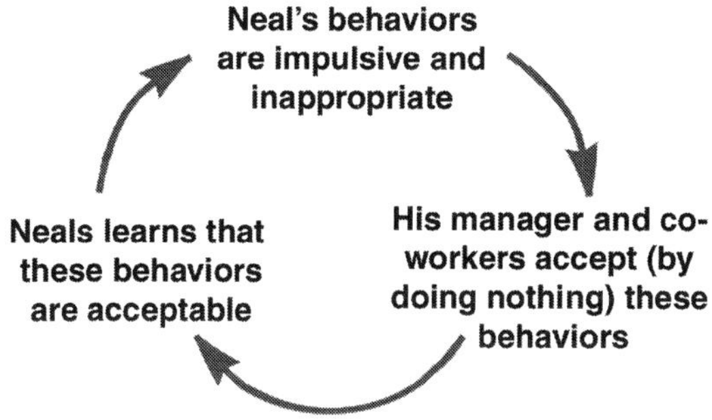

When Neal feels angry, he is likely to express it in Acted-Out ways, because this form of anger is just an extension of his impulsive, inappropriate behaviors. By accepting these behaviors on a daily basis, his manager and co-workers unintentionally create an environment where Neal will be comfortable exhibiting Acted-Out Anger. To prevent Neal from displaying anger in this way, his manager and co-workers can use the anger-management skills *early,* regarding his "ordinary" impulsive and inappropriate behaviors.

Neal's behaviors are performance problems, and his manager has the option of disciplining him and/or sending him to training. But on an informal basis, both his manager and his co-workers can use the following checklist, which is based on the seven anger-management skills, to determine what to say to Neal.

Because Neal tends to exhibit Acted-Out Anger (and the relevant disruptive behaviors of impulsiveness, exaggerated mood swings, and overreactions), his co-workers and manager must focus on making him aware that his behaviors are disruptive and must stop. You will see that these points are made under "Getting to the Real Issues," in both the checklist and the conversation.

Does Neal *want* to work things out?

- We will assume that Neal does.
- If he does not, discipline and other formal steps are the only options.

Acknowledging Feelings

- We have no direct statements from Neal about how he feels.
- It's reasonable to assume he behaves without malice.
- It's reasonable to assume he does not realize his behaviors are disruptive or inappropriate.
- In interactions with him we can acknowledge that he is comfortable and neutral to well-intentioned in his behaviors.

Finding Something in Common

- Working on the same team and in the same department.
- Additional factors such as shared goals and wanting to do well at work.

Getting to the Real Issues

- Neal's behaviors often are disruptive and/or inappropriate.
- He is not aware of this fact.
- He must change these behaviors.

Depersonalizing

- Neal's disruptions do not appear intentional or aimed at specific co-workers or the manager.
- Neal's inappropriate questions do not appear to be aimed at specific customers or to have any motives.
- Comments about the disruptions and inappropriateness must focus on Neal's *behaviors*, and must avoid references to his intentions, personal values, or other personal issues.

Being Direct

- **Talking to the right person.** Co-workers already are talking among themselves about the problem behaviors, so it is time for them (and the manager) to talk to Neal about them.
- **Goals and purposes** are to help Neal do his work more professionally and effectively.
- **Real issues** are the disruptive and inappropriate nature of some of his behaviors, the fact that Neal is unaware of the nature of these behaviors, and the fact that he must change these behaviors.

Letting Go

- This means different things for Neal's co-workers than for the manager, because of the manager's authority.

- The co-workers can informally express their *preferences and hopes* that Neal change his behaviors.
- The manager can take formal steps and *require* Neal to do so, and can *provide* the resources to help him.
- If Neal's behavior does *not* change, his co-workers must work with, deal with, or put up with how Neal acts.
- The manager can discipline or fire Neal.

Based on this checklist, any of his co-workers and the manager can approach Neal in the following ways:

The Co-Workers' Approach

Be Direct	(stating "Neal, I'd like to mention a few ways you can help goals and purposes) the team's overall performance..."
Find Something in Common	"...which we'd both like to see happen."
Acknowledge Feelings	"I know you mean well when you come up with new ideas at meetings, and also when you start asking customers personal questions over the phone."
Getting to the Real Issues	"But what you don't realize is that both behaviors create problems for the rest of us. When we get off the scheduled agenda, we end up losing a lot of time. And customers usually feel offended by the personal questions. These behaviors, and others that are similar, create real problems."

At this point, Neal has a chance to give his perspective, ask questions, add comments, or say whatever else is on his mind. He and the co-worker may—or may not—come up with solutions or agreements.

Letting Go	The co-worker has stated his or her goals and has identified for Neal what he or she sees as the real issues. Now it is up to Neal to decide what he will do regarding this input. The co-worker has done all he or she can.

The Manager's Approach

Letting Go	The co-worker has stated his or her goals and has identified for Neal what he or she sees as the real issues. Now it is up to Neal to decide what he will do regarding this input. The co-worker has done all he or she can.Be Direct (stating "Neal, I've got to point out two performance goals and purposes problems."
Acknowledging Feelings	"I know you mean well..."
Getting to the real issues	"...but two of your behaviors disrupt the team and create problems regarding customers. "The team disruption occurs when you come up with new approaches during a meet-

ing, instead of following the agenda. This throws everyone off track and ends up accomplishing nothing. It would be better to talk about these changes *between* meetings, so everyone can think it over ahead of time.

"The customer problems occur when you start asking personal questions. Customers get very negative when that happens, and we lose the sale. I want you to talk only about the products and how the customers can use them."

Letting Go	The way in which the manager must let go relates to "how much" of Neal's behavior the manager can expect to change. For example, the manager can require, and may get, new behaviors *at work*, but cannot expect to influence the way Neal acts in his personal life.

Regarding work, the manager can keep things informal and see if Neal makes the appropriate changes. If not, the manager has the option of using formal steps: requiring Neal to change his behaviors, providing training and other resources, and firing Neal if necessary.

Based on this checklist, Neal's co-workers (and manager, up to the "Letting Go" step) i*nformally* can use the anger-management skills to influence Neal's behavior. The new Behavior Wheel looks like this:

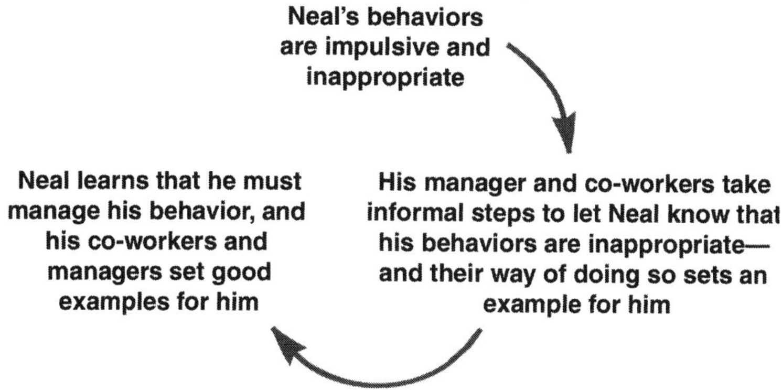

Because Neal exhibits Acted-Out Anger and the accompanying disruptive behaviors, his co-workers and manager emphasized in their approach the need for him to be aware of, and to change, his disruptive behaviors. In addition to improving Neal's general behavior at work, this approach also creates an environment in which Neal is much less likely to exhibit Acted-Out Anger.

By using the seven skills in their day-to-day interactions with Neal—and, of course, each other—the co-workers and manager are role-modeling appropriate ways to deal with problems. At the same time, they are creating an environment where Acted-Out Anger would look more glaringly out of place.

12

Preventing Unconnected Anger

Unconnected Anger means that when co-workers, employees, or managers are held accountable, they angrily resist taking any responsibility for their part of the problem. Even in their day-to-day interactions, when they are *not* angry, these individuals tend to disrupt work by:

- not recognizing how their actions affect others
- not seeing how their actions affect the way others treat them
- repeating the same mistakes.

For example:

Chad thought of himself as good worker and couldn't understand why he got in trouble so much. He just didn't get it when customers complained about his rudeness, or co-workers got tired of correcting his same mistakes over and over, or why some former teammates refused to let him back on their teams. When his manager said he should pay more attention to how he sounded over the phone, he didn't know what the big deal was. He figured it was something about *them*.

The Behavior Wheel looks like this:

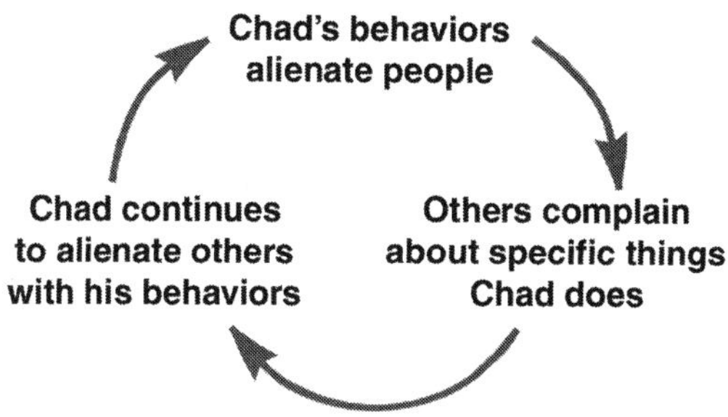

So far, the feedback he's gotten focuses on specific cases. Because Chad tends not to see connections in the first place, he is very *un*likely to take these cases as examples or to learn general lessons from them. Without intending to, and without even knowing it, his co-workers and managers are giving Chad feedback in ways that only reinforce his lack of ability to connect.

Based of the type of anger and the disruptive behaviors Chad displays, his co-workers and manager must emphasize the connections that Chad needs to make. Their approach to him must include the fact that Chad does not own his behaviors, does not realize how they affect others, and is not aware of how his behaviors influence the way others treat him.

By helping Chad "get it" in his daily interactions, his co-workers and manager may be able to lessen his displays of Unconnected Anger—the "worst-case scenario" of his typical behavior.

To discuss these issues with Chad in ways he can use, his co-workers and manager would have to explain the connections to him and help him generalize about each example. You will notice these under "Getting to the Real Issues" in both the checklist and the conversations. Based on the seven anger-management skills, their checklist is:

Does Chad *want* to work things out?

- He may not, because he does not see that his behavior is an issue.

- It's worth a try anyway, because once he starts to understand the connection between his actions and the outcomes, he may become more motivated to work things out.

Acknowledging Feelings

- Chad may feel picked on or left out "for no reason."
- He may be mystified about why he seems not to fit in.
- He clearly does not realize that his own behaviors are causing problems for him.

Finding Something in Common

- Working together.
- Additional factors such as shared goals and wanting to do well at work.

Getting to the Real Issues

- Chad treats others in ways that make them not want to work with him.
- He does not understand that his own behaviors contribute to this problem.
- Feedback has been too situation-related and has not helped Chad understand that individual situations are examples of the fact that his behaviors get negative reactions from others.

Depersonalizing

- Chad's behaviors, and lack of awareness of their impact, appear unintentional on his part.

- Comments about his behaviors must focus on what he *does*, and must avoid references to his intentions, personal values, or other personal issues.

Being Direct

- Talking to the right person. Co-workers and the manager already have tried talking to Chad. This time, they must include Chad's need to generalize.
- Goals and purposes are to help Chad deal more effectively with others and understand the need to do so.
- Real issues are that Chad's inappropriate treatment of others makes them avoid working with him, he is unaware that his behaviors contribute to this problem, and the feedback he's gotten so far has been too specific to help him.

Letting Go

- Co-workers can try to communicate again with Chad, in ways that help him generalize about his behaviors and the ways he affects others.
- If Chad does not change his behaviors, his co-workers must work with, deal with, or put up with how he continues to act.
- His manager can communicate informally, or require Chad to change the way he treats people and also provide resources to help him.
- If Chad's behaviors do not change, the manager can either work with this fact, deal with it, put up with it, or fire him.

Based on the checklist, any of Chad's co-workers and the manager can approach Chad in the following ways:

The Co-Worker's Approach

Be direct (stating goals and purposes)	"Chad, I'm hoping you and I can have a better work relationship. I'd like to talk with you about how we can do that."
Find Something in Common	"It will make work easier for both of us."
Acknowledge Feelings	"You know there have been some problems. And you probably don't realize how your actions have contributed to the problems, or how much of a 'common theme' the problems have."
Getting to the Real Issues	"There are things I have to change also, and we can talk about them too. What I wanted to start out with is that sometimes you treat me in ways that leave me feeling as if you think I'm stupid. It's not just a one-time thing. Even though you do it in different ways each time, I get this general feeling. And when that happens, it makes me want to avoid you, instead of work with you. Do you want to know some of the things you do that make me feel that way?" Chad has the opportunity to learn—but because his co-worker has no authority over him, Chad knows he is not "required" to do anything.
Letting Go	The co-worker has expressed his or her goals and has identified the issues. Now the co-worker must see what Chad decides to do. If

Chad takes part in this conversation, and if his behaviors change, the co-worker will have accomplished his or her goals. If Chad does *not* choose to discuss the issue or change his behaviors, the co-worker must work with, deal with, or put up with these facts.

The Manager's Approach

Be Direct (stating goals and purposes)	"Chad, I'd like to follow up on some things I've told you about your interactions with co-workers and customers. If I can be more clear, you might have an easier time getting along with them. My goal is to improve teamwork..."
Find Something in Common	"...and I think we'd both like for you to feel more comfortable with everyone at work."
Acknowledge Feelings	"I know you don't mean to have trouble with your co-workers, and I also know you're not really sure of how that happens."
Getting to the Real Issues	"I see three problems. First, as I've mentioned in a few conversations with you, some of the ways you deal with people makes them not want to work with you. Second, I don't think you're aware of how your behavior affects them. And third, maybe the most important in some ways, I haven't done a good enough job describing the first two problems to you. Over the next several weeks, I want to spend time helping you see how specific examples

	all have some common points for you to learn. And I'll look into some classes I'd like you to take."
Letting Go	The manager has outlined the problems and the steps to solve them. Once these steps are taken, the manager will monitor Chad's behaviors, give feedback, and decide whether the behaviors meet the manager's expectations. Positive recognition—or termination—will follow. At the same time, the manager cannot expect to affect more than Chad's behavior *at work*—Chad's personal life is outside the manager's authority. And if Chad does not make appropriate changes and the manager fires him, the manager must recognize that he or she did all that was possible in his or her role.

By using the checklist, based on the anger-management skills, the new Behavior Wheel looks like this:

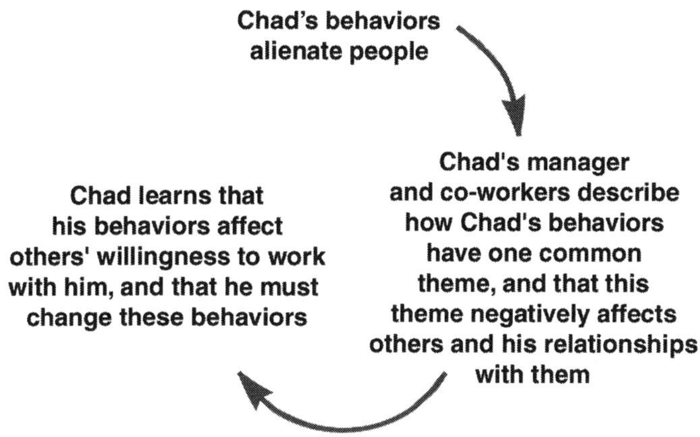

Because Chad does not connect things, he needs these kinds of explanations before he can learn what the problem is. Using the checklist, his manager and co-workers can help Chad improve his work relationships and also create an environment in which Chad is much less likely to exhibit Unconnected Anger.

13

Preventing Self-Centered Anger

In Self-Centered Anger, co-workers, employees, or managers get angry when they can't have their own way. And when they're *not* angry, they tend to disrupt work by:

- focusing only on their own needs, without regard for how their actions affect co-workers or others
- blaming everyone else for their problems
- demanding immediate gratification.

For example:

Melanie thought everyone in her whole department was too demanding. Take the flextime schedule, for example. "Flex" meant flexible, didn't it? So why did her manager still want her to be there between 9:30 and 3:30 every day? And her co-workers were no better. Today they got mad because she took a break right in the middle of the project meeting. Well, her boyfriend has a break at a set time every day, so she had to leave then to have coffee with him. Besides, they're not so dependable either. An hour ago she asked the admin about scheduling her vacation, and the admin still hadn't gotten back to her. The admin had better get back to her soon, or Melanie would have another one of her fits.

Melanie clearly focuses only on her own needs, without any regard for the impact she has on her teammates, her manager, or the company. She misses the point about flextime, is closed to feedback, and doesn't notice the negative effect her absence has on productivity. At this point, the Behavior Wheel looks like this:

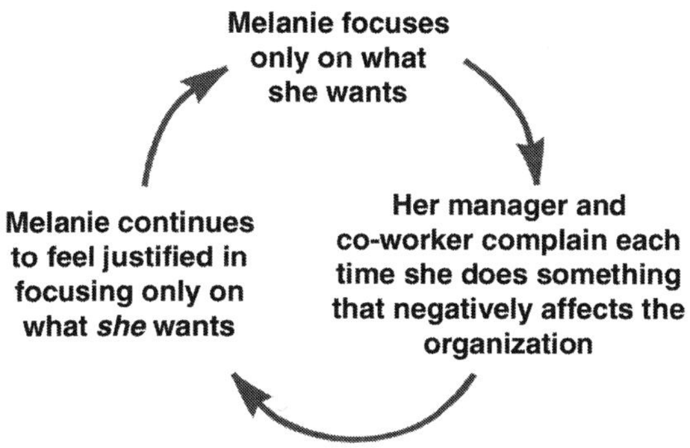

Melanie sees everything at work strictly from the point of view of her own needs and wants. Her manager and co-workers complain, but she is not getting their message. She is so concerned about doing what she wants that she essentially ignores her job duties and other work responsibilities.

Because of Melanie's self-centeredness, her co-workers and manager are more likely to reach her by emphasizing the benefits *to her* of having more regard for what others want. If they can use her self-interest to make her more open to others' needs, she may start to behave in more team-oriented and professional ways. And if Melanie pays more attention to others' needs, she is less likely to exhibit Self-Centered Anger. Their checklist looks like this:

Does Melanie *want* to work things out?

- She certainly wants to follow her own schedule, and she also wants others to be okay about her having her way.
- For now, her desire that others let her have her way provides something to build on. As she sees the payoff for herself in considering others' needs, she may become a little more willing to work things out with people.

Acknowledging Feelings

- Melanie feels entitled to do what she wants at work.
- Melanie feels intruded upon by her co-workers and her manager, who want her to work according to *their* schedule.

Finding Something in Common

- Working together.
- Additional factors such as shared goals and wanting to do well at work.

Getting to the Real Issues

- Melanie wants to follow her own schedule instead of the work schedule.
- She wants her co-workers and manager to support her getting her way.
- She does not understand—and perhaps does not care—that she cannot follow her individual or personal schedule on the job.

Depersonalizing

- Melanie's behaviors and self-centeredness are not directed at anyone in particular. They appear to be her lifestyle and her world view.
- Comments about her behaviors must focus on how *she* can benefit from showing concern about what her co-workers, manager, and others want from her.

Being Direct

- **Talking to the right person.** Co-workers and the manager already have tried talking to Melanie. This time, they must focus on using her self-interest to motivate her to change her behavior.
- **Goals and purposes** are to require Melanie to work within the policies and procedures of the organization.
- **Real issues** are that Melanie wants to follow her own schedule, have others support her doing so, and appears not to care (or understand) that she has to work within the company framework—like everyone else.

Letting Go

- Co-workers can try to communicate again with Melanie in ways that show her how she benefits from considering others' needs. They must avoid talking about her intentions, attitude, or self-centeredness.
- If Melanie does not change her behaviors, her co-workers must work with, deal with, or put up with how she continues to act.

- Her manager can communicate informally, or can require Melanie to include, in her behaviors, other people's needs. The manager also can provide resources to help her.
- If Melanie's behaviors do not change, the manager can either work with this fact, deal with it, put up with it, or fire her.

Based on the checklist, any of Melanie's co-workers and the manager can approach Melanie in the following ways:

The Co-Worker's Approach

Be Direct (stating goals and purposes)	"Melanie, I'd like to talk to you about how you might get more from your job and from us."
Find Something in Common	"Everyone here would gain from this."
Acknowledge Feelings	"I know you have a lot of things going on in your life right now, and a lot of stuff you want to do."
Getting to the Real Issues	"The problem is that some of the things you do at work make it hard for you to get much out of the job. Without realizing it, you sometimes blow people off and then they don't want to help you at work. Can we talk about this?" Melanie has the opportunity to learn. Because her co-worker has no authority over

	her, any changes she makes will be voluntary.
Letting Go	The co-worker has expressed his or her goals and has identified the issues. Now the co-worker must see what Melanie decides to do. If Melanie takes part in this conversation, and if her behaviors change, the co-worker will have accomplished his or her goals. If Melanie does *not* choose to discuss the issue or change her behaviors, the co-worker must work with, deal with, or put up with these facts.

The Manager's Approach

Be Direct (stating goals and purposes)	"Melanie, we need to talk about how you hurt yourself at work when you don't follow the work schedule."
Finding Common Ground	"The team needs your help, and I know you want to get the benefits of doing well in your job."
Acknowledge Feelings	"I know you have a lot going on in your life right now, and sometimes it feels like work gets in the way."
Getting to the Real Issues	"But you won't get what you want from work unless you pay more attention to meeting other people's needs as well as your own. You'd get more cooperation and support by doing this. You may not realize how much

others can help you do well if you help them also. I'd like to give you some specific examples of changes you could make, and how people can be more helpful to you if you make these changes."

Letting Go

The manager has told Melanie what he or she wants and how it will benefit Melanie. Once these steps are taken, the manager will monitor Melanie's behaviors, give feedback, and decide whether the behaviors meet the manager's expectations. The manager can stay informal or can require these changes.

At the same time, the manager cannot expect to affect more than Melanie's behavior *at work*. And if Melanie does not make appropriate changes and the manager fires her, the manager must recognize that he or she did all that was possible in his or her role.

The new Behavior Wheel looks like this:

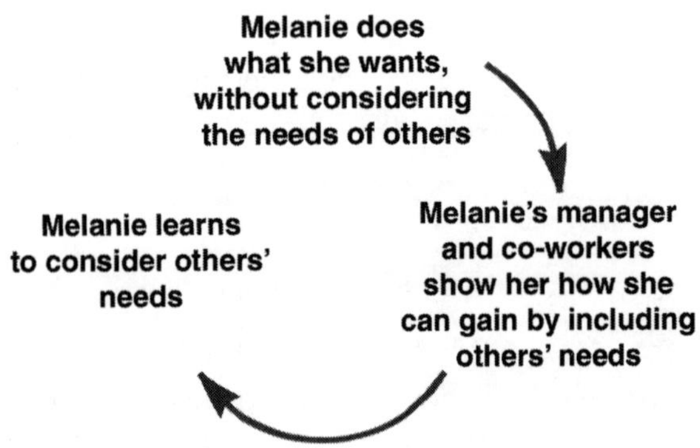

Her manager and co-workers can use Melanie's self-centeredness to motivate her to consider others' needs. Whether she ever *wants* to care about others' needs is difficult to predict. However, as long as her *behaviors* at work change, everyone will benefit. In addition, learning to consider others' needs will reduce the likelihood of Melanie demonstrating Self-Centered Anger at work.

14

PREVENTING UNDERCOVER ANGER

When employees, co-workers, or managers exhibit Acted-Out Anger, Unconnected Anger, or Self-Centered Anger, all of us are very aware of what is happening because these expressions of anger are easy to see (and hear). Undercover Anger, however, is expressed much more behind-the-scenes. Even in their day-to-day behavior, when they're *not* angry, those who exhibit Undercover Anger are disruptive because of their secretive ways. They tend to:

- "get even" with someone (or with the company) without acknowledging that there is a problem
- manipulate others or hint to get what they want
- let things to wrong.

For example:

Bridget didn't want to work overtime anymore. She'd had enough and wanted more time to herself. She also knew that her machine needed to be shut down and fixed, because one of the parts was on the verge of breaking. As an honest person, she would never take any steps to actually break the part. All she had to do was wait while she kept working. And before even her regular hours were over, Bridget's machine suddenly made a grinding noise and stopped. She shut it off and called the maintenance engineers. If the problem was what she thought it was, Bridget figured it would take at least 30 hours to fix it. She wouldn't have to come back until the day after tomorrow. She waited until she left the building before she smiled to herself. She'd gotten away with this before, and she needed the break.

Although Bridget did not actively destroy anything—as, for example, someone displaying Acted-Out Anger would do—she let things go wrong by failing to take appropriate action. Because her actions are covert, no one can prove that she did it on purpose. Yet she disrupts work by slowing production and adding pressure to everyone else's workload. The Behavior Wheel looks like this:

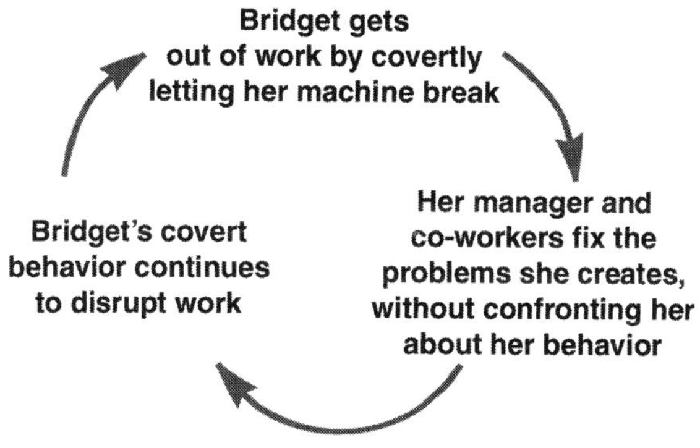

Bridget gets away with her disruptive behavior because it is so hard to prove that she let her machine break down. While active behavior is visible, it is hard to accuse her of purposely being passive by not calling in time.

If Bridget's co-workers and manager want to influence her behavior, they'll have to find ways to bring her secret actions out into the open. Only then can she be held responsible for not doing what she should. Their checklist looks like this:

Does Bridget *want* to work things out?

- Not likely. The fact that her behaviors are secretive indicates that she does not want them to be discovered, brought out in the open, or discussed.
- The fact that she's done this before decreases the likelihood of her wanting to work things out openly.
- At the same time, we can assume she wants to keep her job. This may be the only motivation she would have to work things out.

Acknowledging Feelings

- Bridget feels annoyed because of the long hours.
- She generally may feel afraid of saying what she means.
- She may feel afraid that management would not listen, or would look down on her, if she complains about the hours.

Finding Something in Common

- The need for everyone to work together.
- The need to maintain equipment properly.
- The desire that Bridget keeps her job.

Getting to the Real Issues

- Bridget purposely let her machine break down.
- She did so in passive, secretive ways.

- She has to actively take care of her machine.
- She must be more open and direct about things that bother her, instead of dealing with them in covert ways.

Depersonalizing

- Passively letting the machine break down is unacceptable at work, even if it's "Bridget's nature" to express herself this way.
- Dealing with issues (such as the long hours) covertly is unacceptable at work, even if it's "her nature" to do so.
- Her co-workers and manager must focus on her behavior and *not* her intentions. Although this is true for all disruptive behaviors, it is particularly important when the behavior is secretive. Otherwise, there is a risk of sounding as if you're "mind-reading."

Being Direct

- **Talking to the right person.** No one has spoken to Bridget yet about her covert behaviors. It is time for her manager to address the performance problems she is demonstrating. Co-workers must focus on the impact her behavior has on them.
- **Goals and purposes** are to help Bridget speak openly and stop acting in covert ways.
- **Real issues** are that Bridget failed to maintain her machine properly, that she secretly let it fail, and that she appears to be acting covertly because of problems regarding work.

Letting Go

- Co-workers can let her know how they, and their productivity, were affected by her machine breaking down.
- Co-workers then have to work with, deal with, or put up with the action she takes. They also have the option of letting the manager know if her behavior continues to affect them, and productivity, negatively.
- Her manager can talk to Bridget informally, or can require her behaviors to change. The manager also can provide resources, such as training and/or counseling.
- If Bridget's behavior does not improve, the manager can either accept this fact or take disciplinary actions leading to termination.

Based on this checklist, Bridget's co-workers and manager can talk to Bridget in the following ways:

The Co-Worker's Approach

Be Direct (stating goals and purposes)	"Bridget, I had to work 18 hours because you let your machine break down. I want to tell you how much of a problem that caused for everyone, and also find ways we can help each other."
Find Something in Common	"If we can find these ways, it would make work easier and better for all of us."
Acknowledge Feelings	"I know how fed up you are with the long hours. I also know you don't want to be seen as a whiner."

Get to the Real Issues	"This is the second time it's happened, and the first time was also when we'd been working extra hours. Some people think you purposely let it break down because you wanted to get out of working. We wish you'd do something different instead of taking it out on us. If you don't want to say anything to management, talk to the team down here—we can probably work something out about scheduling."
Letting go	The co-worker has let Bridget know that the team is aware of what she's doing, and they're willing to figure out ways to resolve the problem if she'll be open to them about being bothered by the hours. If Bridget chooses to be more open with the team, it may work. But if she chooses not to, the co-worker must recognize that he or she did everything possible. The co-workers must then work with, deal with, or put up with Bridget's behaviors.

The Manager's Approach

Be Direct (stating goals and purposes)	"Bridget, I want to talk with you about several problems I have regarding your maintenance of your machine."
Find Something in Common	"Both you and I want you to stay in this job."

Acknowledge Feelings	"I know you have problems with the long hours. And I know it's possible that you may have overlooked the condition of your machine because you're tired."
Getting to the Real Issues	"But I'm also wondering if you're trying to tell me something about the long hours, without directly telling me. I'd like to talk to you about two issues—this second breakdown of your machine, and what might be behind it. There may be some need for technical training, and perhaps training in communicating more directly. Let's schedule a time to discuss these issues." Without accusing her, the manager has let Bridget know that he or she is aware of the possibility of covert behavior as a form of "getting even." The manager must remain unemotional and open to be effective in this situation.
Letting Go	In this case, the manager already has chosen the formal, instead of informal, approach—he or she is *requiring* that Bridget change her behaviors. The manager will give Bridget a chance to speak openly and maintain her machine properly, and to get help doing both on a regular basis. If Bridget accepts this opportunity, the manager will monitor both how well she maintains her machine and how openly she discusses work issues that bother her.

Bridget may choose to leave the job instead of having the discussion or making the changes. If so, the manager must realize that he or she did all that was possible in this case.

If Bridget takes part in the discussion, and improves these behaviors, the manager can recognize and reinforce the changes. If Bridget stays but does not change her behaviors, the manager is likely to terminate her. If so, the manager again must recognize that he or she did everything possible in this work situation.

If Bridget stays and makes the changes, the new Behavior Wheel will look like this:

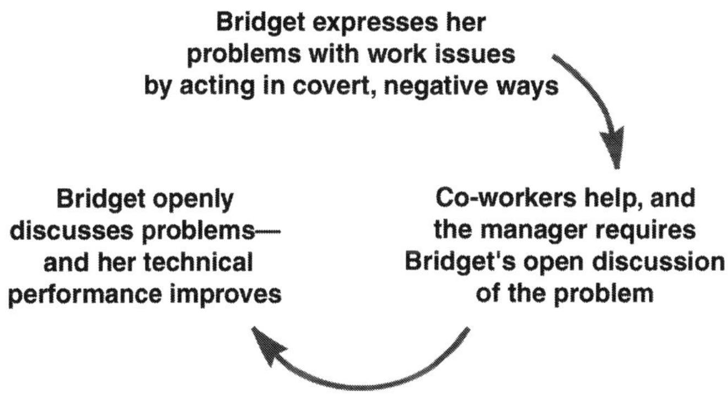

Co-workers and the manager have to address both issues: Bridget's poor maintenance of her machine, and the covert nature of the ways in which she failed to maintain it. If Bridget stays and makes the changes, her tendency to exhibit Undercover Anger also will diminish.

15

Preventing Rigid Anger

Co-workers, employees, and managers who exhibit Rigid Anger do not acknowledge alternatives, the need for compromise, or the value of negotiation. Even when they're *not* angry, they tend to disrupt the workplace in the following ways:

- demanding perfection—of themselves and others
- thinking and behaving in "either-or" ways
- trying to control the way others do things.

For example:

Carl was glad the manager finally put him on this team, because Carl knew that his engineering background was exactly what the project needed. Everyone else on the team was either in sales or computers, and that explained why they couldn't push this project along. As soon as he showed up at the next meeting, he started out by telling them how he would show them the right way to get this project done.

"I looked over all the plans," he said, "and I saw what's holding you guys up. In fact," he said, standing up and walking towards the flipchart, "I can show it to you right now." A few people sat quietly, one person left the room, and everyone else, obviously annoyed, sat but paid no attention as Carl talked.

Even if Carl is correct and has useful information to share with the team, he alienates everyone by behaving in ways that are inflexible, controlling, and right-wrong. Even worse, this is only the first time he's met with the team. The Behavior Wheel looks like this:

Carl interrupted the team meeting, and no one has stopped him. He believes he's doing the right thing, and everyone's silence—along with Carl's failure to see their annoyance—reinforces him.

If the team members and Carl's manager want to influence his behavior, they will have to appeal to his desire to help the team and then show him that he is, in fact, hindering it. Their checklist looks like this:

Does Carl *want* to work things out?

- He very likely does. Carl's style alienates the team—but his goal is to help them.
- Carl is unaware of what his style is and how it negatively affects others.
- Carl does not pick up the feedback he could get from others' responses.

Acknowledging Feelings

- Carl is intent on helping the team.
- Carl believes he has something to offer that the team needs.
- He is oblivious to how he comes across.
- He thinks he is helping the team.

Finding Something in Common

- The goal of making the team more effective.
- The team's need for Carl's engineering skills and his desire to help them.

Getting to the Real Issues

- Carl's style is too forceful, rigid, and either-or for the team.
- He should learn more about what the team has done so far, before he gives input about what they should do.
- He is unaware of the impact his behavior had on the team and on his ability to help the team.

Depersonalizing

- Carl's good intentions do not make his behaviors acceptable.
- The team members and Carl's manager must help Carl separate his good intentions from his inappropriate behaviors.

Being Direct

- **Talking to the right person.** Team members most likely have talked among themselves about Carl's behavior. Now they should talk to him about what they need from him. Carl's manager must give him feedback and guidance.

- **Goals and purposes** are to help Carl change his behaviors so the team can benefit from his behaviors.
- **Real issues** are that Carl's style is too rigid and controlling, he should learn more about the team's work before he suggests anything, and he needs to learn how to take feedback from others' responses to him.

Letting Go

- Team members can tell Carl how he can help them more by treating them differently.
- Team members must work with, deal with, or put up with Carl's behavior if he does not make changes.
- His manager can either give Carl informal guidance or require him to change his behavior. In either case, the manager also can provide resources that will help Carl.
- If Carl does not change his behaviors, his manager can either accept his current behavior or remove him from the team. Termination would not be appropriate if the only problems relate to the team.

Based on this checklist, Carl's teammates and manager can talk to Carl in these ways:

The Co-Worker's Approach

Being Direct (stating goals and purposes)	"Carl, you have a lot to offer the team. But we are having trouble with how forcefully you're starting out, and I'd like to talk to you about that."

Finding Something in Common	"All of us want the team to succeed."
Acknowledge Feelings	"We all know you want to help us. And we know you have a lot to offer."
Getting to the Real Issues	"But when you came in and started telling us what we were doing wrong, before you even knew what we'd done, a lot of us just shut you out. We need you to treat us the same way we treat you—*all* the team members have something to offer."
Letting Go	The team member has explained the problem to Carl and has given him ideas about how to work better with the team. If Carl does not change his behaviors, the team member cannot blame himself or herself. The entire team must either work with Carl's behavior, deal with it—perhaps by requesting that he be removed from the team—or put up with it.

The Manager's Approach

Be Direct (stating goals and purposes)	"Carl, I have to talk with you about some of the things you did at your first team meeting. Let's do that right now."
Find Something in Common	"Both you and I know you have a lot to offer the team."

Acknowledge Feelings	"I know you mean well and are trying to help them."
Getting to the Point	"But you came across as very controlling, and this was only your first meeting with them. Even if what you have to say is right, they got a bad impression because of how you said it. I'd suggest that you first take some time to learn what they've done so far. Also, you'd do well to pay more attention to how others react to you. If you'd done that, you would have known you were coming on too strong." The manager has chosen to guide Carl informally. if Carl does not change his behavior, the manager still has the option of removing him from the team and having him meet with specific team members individually to share his information.
Letting Go	If Carl does not behave appropriately, the manager can come up with other ways of getting Carl's information to the team without them having to deal with his behavior. In all situations, the manager has done everything possible with Carl.

If Carl makes the appropriate changes, the Behavior Wheel looks like this:

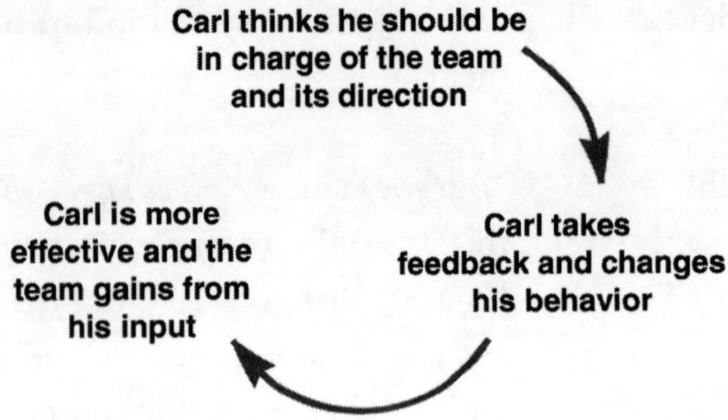

If Carl learns to look for feedback and adjust his behaviors, he will be an effective team member. He also will be less likely, when he's angry, to exhibit Rigid Anger.

16

Preventing Escapist Anger

With Escapist Anger, co-workers, employees, and managers lie or use drugs or alcohol, and are into denial about their anger and their ways of dealing with anger. Even when they're *not* angry, they tend to disrupt the workplace by:

- lying
- avoiding situations they find stressful (including job duties, deadlines, and other work requirements)
- distancing others
- exaggerating their part of a successful event
- minimizing their responsibility for failures

For example:

> Everyone was discouraged when Juan was put in charge of the team. They'd hoped to really accomplish something on this project, but with Juan in charge it just wouldn't happen. When two team members went to ask him a question, Juan was asleep at his desk. It was no wonder that there were problems with this project!

When the team started meeting without Juan, things picked up and they achieved the goals on time. The company held a big dinner, celebrating the team's accomplishments. The team members felt proud until Juan stood up and said, "Thank you, I am honored by your appreciation. It was a hard task, and I worked hard to accomplish it. Oh, and thank you to the team members."

Juan's exaggerated sense of his contribution only added to the team's frustration about Juan literally sleeping on the job. The Behavior Wheel looks like this:

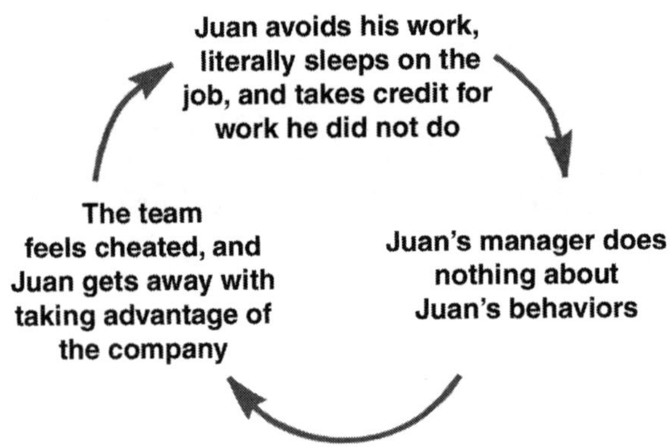

The fact that Juan gets away with this behavior can discourage not only the team members, but the entire organization. Without intending to, management conveys the message that something other than good work gets rewarded, and Escapist behavior will go unnoticed or undisciplined. When Juan gets angry, he will assume that he will get away with anything he does. If he is drunk, or on drugs, at the time, he will not remember doing anything and will take no responsibility for his actions.

If Juan's teammates and manager want to influence his behavior, they will have to make Juan deal with reality by putting consequences to his behavior. Their checklist looks like this:

Does Juan want to work things out?

- Juan is not aware there is a problem, so he is unaware of the need to work anything out.
- Even when he becomes aware of a problem, he is not likely to accept much responsibility for it.

Acknowledging Feelings

- Juan is very likely out of touch with his own feelings, due to alcohol and/or drugs.
- His denial makes it hard to get through to him.
- He wants to believe that everything is all right and that he does a good job.

Finding Something in Common

- It's reasonable to assume that Juan wants to keep his job.
- It's also reasonable to assume that if Juan's behavior can be corrected, the company also would prefer that he keep his job.

Getting to the Real Issues

- Juan fell asleep at his desk.
- He failed to lead the team or do his work on the team project.
- There are underlying causes of these problems.
- These causes must be addressed.

Depersonalizing

- Because of his denial, Juan is not as aware of his problems as his manager and teammates are.
- Juan is not "aiming" his behavior at anyone.
- Juan's behavior at work must change, even though he doesn't "mean" to do what he does.

Being Direct

- **Talking to the right person.** Team members can give Juan input about who really did the work on the project. Juan's manager must give him feedback and require changes.
- **Goals and purposes** are to change Juan's behaviors and performance at work, and to have him address the underlying issues so his positive changes will last.
- **Real issues** are that Juan has behavior and performance problems and that he must address the underlying causes.

Letting Go

- Team members can give Juan feedback about who really did the work, how they felt when he took the credit, and how they needed his help.
- Once they have told Juan this, they must work with, deal with, or put up with Juan's behavior if he does not change.
- Juan's manager can require Juan to change his behavior and to get the help he needs to do so. The manager also can provide the resources to help Juan.
- If Juan does not change his behavior, the manager must terminate him.

Based on this checklist, Juan's teammates and manager can talk to Juan in these ways:

The Co-Worker's Approach

Being Direct (stating goals and purposes)	"Juan, you were in charge of the team. But I have a problem with how you handled the team. Can we talk about this?"
Finding Something in Common	"Everyone wants to get recognition for what they do."
Acknowledge Feelings	"I know that you believe you did a lot of the work on this project."
Getting to the Real Issues	"But the truth is that everyone else on the team did the work. You really didn't do anything. And on top of that, at the dinner you took most of the credit. I'd like to see you give more recognition to the team members."
Letting Go	The team member has described the problem and asked for what he or she wants. If Juan does not give credit to the team, the team member must accept the fact that he or she did everything possible regarding getting Juan to do something. Regarding the issue of credit for the team, the team member can still go to Juan's manager. Regarding Juan's behavior—refusing to give credit—only the manager can intervene.

The Manager's Approach

Be Direct (stating goals and purposes)	"Juan, you've made some serious errors regarding the team project. I have to talk with you about where to go from here."
Find Something in Common	"We both know you were supposed to lead the team."
Acknowledge Feelings	"And I know you think you did a good job."
Getting to the Real Issues	"But in fact, it was the team members who did everything. You didn't do your part of the work, you even were asleep at your desk, and you didn't lead the team at all. They had to meet without you to finish the project. And even worse, you took all the credit at the dinner. All of these behaviors are unacceptable. Unfortunately, these behaviors on your part happen too often. I'm going to require you to take appropriate responsibility, carry out your work duties, and produce the expected results. I'm also requiring you to go to the Employee Assistance Program, so they can help you identify and work on the causes of your inappropriate behaviors."

The manager has put these requirements on Juan. If Juan does not go to the Employee Assistance Program, or if his behavior does not change even if he does go, the manager will terminate him. The manager has done everything possible with Juan.

If Juan makes the appropriate changes, the Behavior Wheel will look like this:

In this case, Juan is likely to need a lot of help—and also need to do a lot of work on himself—making the required changes. If he does, he will be much more effective at work. And he also will be much less likely to exhibit Escapist Anger when he's angry.

17

Preventing Shocking Anger

In Shocking Anger, the co-workers, employees, or managers express their anger in ways that are extreme or out of character. Even when they're *not* angry, these individuals tend to disrupt the workplace by:

- behaving in extreme or flamboyant ways
- changing moods suddenly and dramatically
- suddenly going from performing well to performing very poorly
- going from reliable attendance to erratic attendance
- suddenly acting in ways that are inconsistent with their overall personality.

As an example:

> Elise always worked in a steady, dependable way. She wasn't the fastest, but her work was consistently error-free and she had never missed a day of work. So everyone was surprised when she didn't show up on Monday and didn't call in. When she got there on Tuesday, everyone was surprised to see that she had trouble concentrating on her work. She made a lot of

errors that day, and just didn't seem like herself. Her co-workers figured she'd had problems at home, and her manager worried that she was looking for another job.

The sudden changes in Elise's attendance, performance, and behavior are out of character for her, and her co-workers and manager make assumptions about the reasons. The Behavior Wheel looks like this

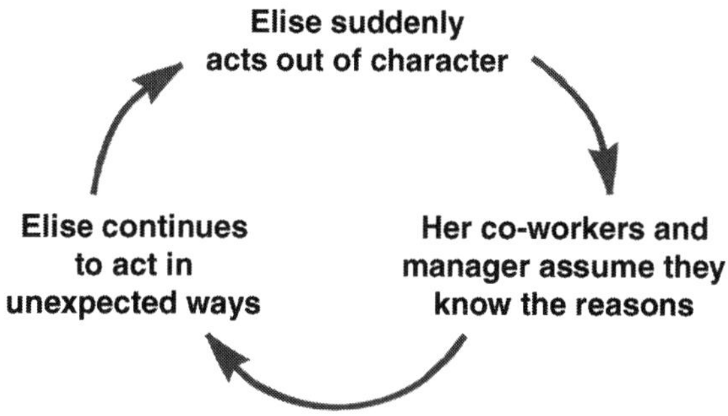

Extreme or out-of-character behavior can come from personal, physical, psychological, emotional, and other causes. In addition to hurting productivity and upsetting her co-workers and manager, Elise's behavior also may indicate that she needs help. If her need for help is ignored, Elise's situation could worsen and, when she's angry, she could exhibit Shocking Anger.

If Elise's co-workers and manager want to influence her behavior, they will have to make her aware of the changes they observed. By doing so, they also will be enabling her to get any help she might need. Their checklist looks like this:

Does Elise *want* to work things out?

- It is reasonable to assume she does.
- Her history as a good worker supports the idea that her behavior changes are due to something outside her control.

Acknowledging Feelings

- Elise may be unaware of the changes in her behavior.
- It also is possible that Elise feels uncomfortable, disoriented, or even fearful.

Finding Something in Common

- Everyone wants Elise to work and behave the way she usually does.
- Everyone wants Elise to feel better.

Getting to the Real Issues

- Elise's performance and behaviors have changed suddenly and for the worse.
- She may not be aware of this fact.
- These changes may indicate that she needs help in some ways.

Depersonalizing

- It does not appear that Elise made these changes intentionally or even knowingly.
- Her new behaviors are not directed at anyone.

Being Direct

- **Talking to the right person.** Co-workers and the manager must tell Elise what they observe.
- **Goals and purposes** are to alert Elise about the changes and help her work and act like her normal self.

- **Real issues** are that Elise's behavior has changed suddenly and for the worse, she may not be aware of this fact, and she may need some help.

Letting Go

- Co-workers can tell Elise what they see, and how concerned they are.
- They must work with, deal with, or put up with whatever Elise decides to do. They cannot "make" her get help, and only the manager can require improvements in behavior.
- Her manager can informally tell her what he or she sees, and can suggest that she get help from the Employee Assistance Program or other counseling resources.
- If Elise refuses to get help and/or does not improve her behavior, the manager can require her to do so. However, in this case, the informal approach is most likely to be effective.
- The manager has to recognize that he or she has done everything possible to help Elise.

Based on this checklist, the conversations can go like this:

The Co-Worker's Approach

Be Direct (stating goals and purposes)	"Elise, I'm worried about you. You're not acting like your usual self. What's wrong?"
Find something in common	"We're confused about what's happening. You may be also."

Acknowledge Feelings	"I wonder if you're not feeling like your usual self."
Get to the Real Issues	"You've never been absent before, and your work wasn't as good as usual. Do you know what you need?"
Let Go	Elise may or may not share information or feelings with the co-worker. The co-worker has done all he or she can to be available.

The Manager's Approach

Be Direct (stating goals and purposes)	"Elise, your performance and behavior are very different from usual. I'd like to hear more about what's happening..."
Find Something in Common	"...although you may not know either."
Acknowledge Feelings	"Sometimes things can happen that are very confusing. I want to assure you that we'll help all we can."
Getting to the Real Issues	"You've never been absent before, and it was unlike you not to call. And when you came on Tuesday, you didn't perform as well as usual. I'm wondering if it's something about work and if you'd like to see the Employee Assistance Program counselor."

Letting Go	The manager has tried to be helpful to Elise. If her behavior does not improve, it could become a performance issue. The manager has done all that is possible.

If Elise gets back to her usual actions and performance, the Behavior Wheel will look like this:

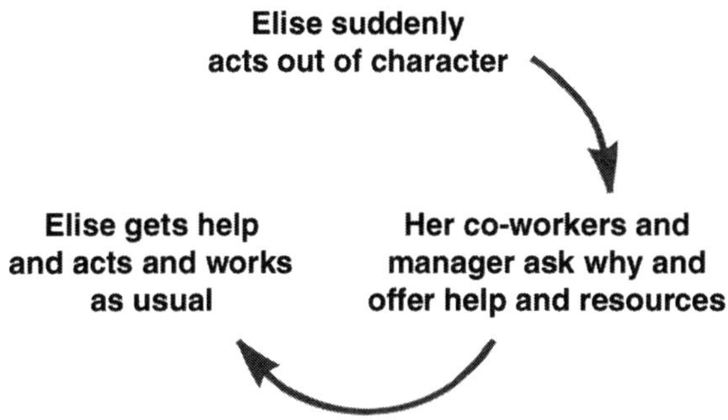

In this situation, Elise is likely to get help regarding private, as well as work-related, issues. In addition, when she's angry, she is much less likely to exhibit Shocking Anger.

18

PREVENTING STRANGE ANGER

Employees, co-workers, and managers who exhibit Strange Anger carry out their anger in ways that are bizarre and may not make sense to most of us. Even when they are *not* angry, these individuals may disrupt the workplace by:

- being extremely remote and withdrawn
- being suspicious of others
- becoming obsessed with an idea or another individual
- losing touch with reality.

For example:

> Ted worked in the back room and he liked it that way. No noise, no one bothering him most of the time. His co-workers liked it that way also, because Ted was hard to be around. He rarely responded when someone talked to him, and he often seemed to be listening to something that no one else heard. At times, he was heard talking to himself.
>
> Now there was a problem. Ted was supposed to ship a product out last week, but the product never got to the customer. The customer was angry and the manager and co-workers were trying to find out what happened.

"Ted, do you recall the package that was supposed to be shipped to Los Angeles last week?" one of the co-workers asked. "There's no record of it having been shipped."

Ted looked at him. "I sent everything out that was supposed to go out," Ted said. "But my enemies may have erased the records."

Bewildered, the co-worker asked the manager, "What do we do now?"

The manager shrugged his shoulders and sighed.

Ted's unusual behavior disrupts work and confuses his co-workers and manager. The Behavior Wheel looks like this:

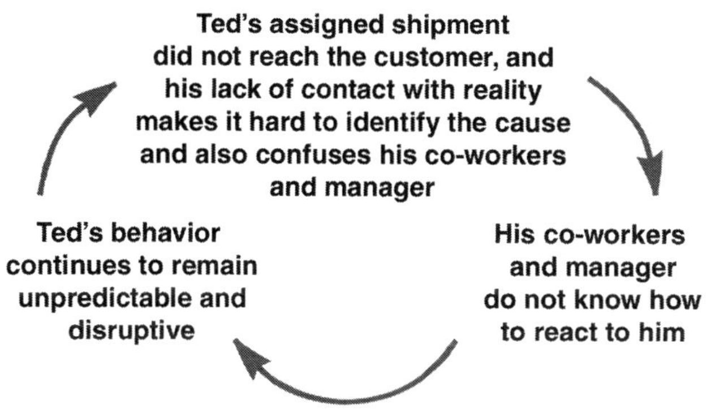

Behaviors that are remote, suspicious, out of touch with reality, and unusual in other ways can come from many sources. It is *not* the role of co-workers or managers to diagnose or treat this behavior. It *is* the role of managers to make sure that all employees do their work and that when they exhibit these types of behaviors, they get help that enables them to perform their jobs. If the manager and co-workers ignore Ted's behavior, his behavior could worsen and, if he gets angry, he is likely to exhibit Strange Anger.

If Ted's co-workers and manager want to influence Ted's behavior, they will have to be supportive and objective at the same time. Their checklist looks like this:

Does Ted *want* to work things out?

- It is reasonable to assume he does. From Ted's point of view, he is doing his job and facing problems.
- Most of the time, he performs his job at an acceptable level.

Acknowledging Feelings

- From Ted's perspective, he is doing his job and "enemies" sometimes remove the records.
- Ted is not likely to be aware that he is sometimes out of touch with reality.

Finding Something in Common

- Everyone wants to do a good job.
- Everyone wants all the co-workers to accomplish their goals.

Getting to the Real Issues

- The customer did not get the product, and it is possible that Ted did not ship it out.
- Steps must be put in place to make sure that all shipments, by all employees, get out.
- Ted believes he did ship it out, but his "enemies" removed the record of the shipment.
- Ted's perceptions sometimes are inaccurate.

Depersonalizing

- Ted is not behaving disruptively on purpose—or even knowingly.
- Ted's disruptive behaviors are not aimed at anyone.
- Ted may have shipped the product, as he said he did.

Being Direct

- **Talking to the right person.** Co-workers and the manager must discuss, with Ted, the problem regarding the product that did not arrive.
- **Goals and purposes** are to correct the mistake and find ways to make sure it doesn't happen again.
- **Real issues** are the need for shipments getting to customers, finding out what the problem was with the shipment for which Ted was responsible, and finding ways to make sure all shipments get out as they should.

Letting Go

- The co-workers can try to find out whether the product was shipped and if it was, why it did not get to the customer. They also can find out what happened to the record of the shipment.
- They cannot address Ted's performance or behaviors, because they do not have the authority to do either.
- Depending on whether or not Ted shipped the product, and on what happened to the record of the shipment if he did, the manager may have to address a performance problem.

- The manager may address Ted's behaviors *only* to the extent that the behaviors interfere with, or disrupt, work. At the same time, the manager can offer—and even require that Ted use—resources such as training and/or the Employee Assistance Program or other forms of counseling or support.

Based on this checklist, the conversations can go like this:

The Co-Worker's Approach

Be Direct (stating goals and purposes)	"I'd like to find out what happened to that shipment. Can we talk about it, so we can figure out where it is and what happened to the record of it?"
Find Something in Common	"We all make mistakes, and sometimes things get messed up. This could happen to any of us, so we need to work together to figure out what it was."
Acknowledge Feelings	"I know you believe you shipped it, and that someone who doesn't like you removed the record of the shipment. And that very well may be what happened."
Get to the Real Issues	"That's what we've got to find out—who did what, and what happened. We have to make sure it doesn't happen again, to any of us, and that's why we need to find out."
Letting Go	The co-worker has tried to make this a department, not individual, problem. He or she

cannot control Ted's willingness to cooperate. If Ted does not cooperate, the co-worker has to work with this decision, deal with it (including asking the manager to intervene) or put up with it.

The Manager's Approach

Be Direct (stating goals and purposes)	"Ted, we have to find out whether you shipped the product, what happened to the shipment and the records if you did, and what the circumstances were if you did not. The reason is to find out why the product didn't get to the customer. When we know the reasons, we can make sure it doesn't happen again."
Find Something in Common	"Shipment problems can happen to anyone. That's why we have to use this as an example we can learn from."
Acknowledge Feelings	"You think you remember shipping it, and you think someone removed the records."
Getting to the Real Issues	"Right now, I want to focus on the shipment itself. I need to have you work with the rest of the department in tracing exactly what happened that day. I also need to know if you suspect that one of your co-workers removed the records, and what you think his or her motives were."

By asking about who Ted thinks removed the records, the manager is trying to get Ted to focus on reality. Ted either will have an individual in mind, will refuse to name anyone, or will refuse to answer. In any of these cases, the manager has taken Ted's suspicions seriously, given Ted a chance to name a real suspect if there is one, and helped Ted focus on what's real.

Letting Go

The manager is focusing only on work-related issues. If there is a performance problem—such as an error Ted made in the shipment—the manager can arrange for training. If Ted's response includes a reference to imagined "suspects"—if he says, for example, "They're just my enemies. I know who they are, but you don't"), the manager can refer Ted to the Employee Assistance Program or other source of counseling. If Ted's perceptions continue to interfere with his performance, the manager can *require* that he get counseling. In all these situations, the manager addresses behaviors only as they relate to work. He or she saves the diagnosing, interpreting, and helping for the counselors.

The manager also may have to establish a method by which all shipments can be double-checked, for all employees. In addition, the manager must recognize that he or she can get help for Ted in focusing on reality *at work*. Although Ted's personal life may

> improve as well—and although the manager may be pleased if it does—that is not the manager's goal or purpose.

If Ted works with the team, and gets the counseling he needs, the Behavior Wheel will look like this:

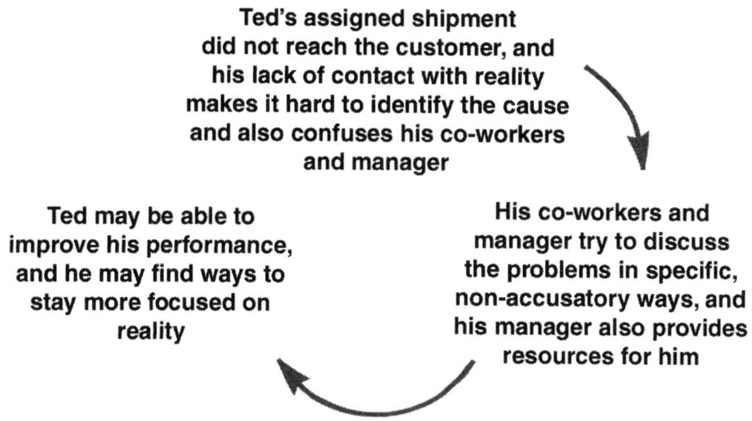

Through this process, Ted's performance and reality-base can improve. At the same time, his co-workers' and manager's actions have made it less likely that Ted will exhibit Strange Anger.

19

You Can Manage Anger & Conflict

You know that anger and conflict are problems at work and that too often, they are not managed well—or at all. Now, you have tools that can help you manage your own anger and deal more effectively with others' anger: a map that identifies eight inappropriate ways your co-workers, employees, and manager deal with their anger, and seven skills with which you can address all eight ways.

In *Acted-Out Anger,* co-workers, employees, or managers make it clear they are angry, but do nothing to solve the problem.

In *Irresponsible Anger,* they take no responsibility for their actions and blame others for their failings.

In *Self-Centered Anger,* they act only in their own self-interest, regardless of the impact they have on their co-workers, the company, or customers.

In *Undercover Anger,* they get even without making it clear there was a problem in the first place.

In *Rigid Anger,* they are extremely controlling and demand to have things their way.

In *Escapist Anger,* they deny—and lie about—the reality of their own problem behavior and feel picked on "for no reason."

In *Shocking Anger*, they behave in ways that are very much out of character for them.

In *Strange Anger,* they are dealing with their own reality and their behavior appears bizarre to others.

You have seven skills that will work with all eight inappropriate expressions of anger:

- *Decide* whether you and the other person really want to work things out with each other.
- *Be direct* about going to the appropriate person, stating your goals and purposes.
- *Acknowledge feelings,* before getting to facts or issues.
- *Find something in common,* to keep both of you motivated to work things out.
- *Depersonalize* and look at the situation from a number of possible angles.
- *Get to the real issues,* instead of getting lost in the details.
- *Let go,* once you have done everything you can.

You can use these skills both *before* co-workers, employees, or managers get angry, and at the moment they *get* angry.

Whether you, your own co-workers, employees, and managers already are too angry, or this has not become a problem yet, you're ready to do your part in managing anger and conflict where you work.

About the Author

D Dr. Lynne McClure is nationally-recognized as one of the leading experts in managing high-risk behaviors in the workplace. A consultant, expert witness, author, and speaker, Dr. McClure has been featured by *CNN NewsStand, CBS This Morning,* Fox News Channel's *The O'Reilly Factor, U.S. News & World Report, USA Today,* The Peter Drucker Foundation's *Leader to Leader,* Franklin Covey's *Priorities,* and other prominent media. Author of *Risky Business: Managing Employee Violence in the Workplace,* she is president of McClure Associates, Inc. in Phoenix. Clients include Fortune 500 corporations and midsized firms. Dr. McClure can be reached at:

LMcClure@McClureAssociates.com
480-829-6801
www.McClureAssociates.com

Index

Business and Career Resources

Contact Impact Publications for a free annotated listing of resources or visit the World Wide Web for a complete listing of resources: **www.impactpublications.com**. The following books are available directly from Impact Publications. (Please add shipping—$5.00 plus 8 percent of total).

IMPACT PUBLICATIONS
9104 Manassas Drive, Suite N
Manassas Park, VA 20111-5211
Tel 1-800/361-1055, 703/361-7300, or Fax 703/335-9486
Quick and easy online ordering: ***www.impactpublications.com***

Qty.	Titles	Price	Total
	The CareerSavvy Series		
______	100 Top Internet Job Sites	12.95	______
______	101 Hiring Mistakes Employers Make...Avoid Them	15.95	______
______	Anger and Conflict in the Workplace	15.95	______
______	The Best 100 Web Sites for HR Professionals	13.95	______
______	The Difficult Hire	14.95	______
______	Recruit and Retain the Best	14.95	______
______	Savvy Interviewing	10.95	______
______	The Savvy Resume Writer	12.95	______
	Hiring & Retention		
______	45 Effective Ways for Hiring Smart!	24.95	______
______	96 Great Interview Questions to Ask Before You Hire	16.95	______
______	Complete Reference Checking Handbook	29.95	______
______	Directory of Executive Recruiters 2000	44.95	______
______	Employer's Guide to Recruiting on the Internet	24.95	______
______	Finding and Keeping Great Employees	24.95	______
______	High Impact Hiring	34.95	______
______	Hire With Your Head	29.95	______
______	Love 'Em or Lose 'Em	17.95	______
______	Manager's Book of Questions	12.95	______
______	Unofficial Guide to Hiring & Firing Employees	16.00	______
______	Verify Those Credentials	19.95	______
	Motivating & Energizing Your Workforce		
______	1001 Ways to Energize Employees	12.00	______
______	1001 Ways to Reward Employees	12.00	______
______	Bringing Out the Best in People	21.95	______
______	Getting Employees to Fall in Love with Your Company	17.95	______
______	Passionate Organization	24.95	______
______	Take This Job and Thrive	14.95	______